The Hulton Getty Picture Collection

1930s

The Hulton Getty Picture Collection

19**30**s

Decades of the 20th Century
Dekaden des 20. Jahrhunderts
Décennies du XXᵉ siècle

Nick Yapp

KÖNEMANN

First published in 1998 by Könemann Verlagsgesellschaft mbH, Bonner Straße 126, D-50968 Köln

©1998 Könemann Verlagsgesellschaft mbH. Photographs ©1998 Hulton Getty Picture Collection Limited

This book was produced by The Hulton Getty Picture Collection Limited,
Unique House, 21–31 Woodfield Road, London W9 2BA

For Könemann:
Production director: Detlev Schaper
Managing editor: Sally Bald
Project editor: Susanne Hergarden
Production assistant: Nicola Leurs
German translation: Angela Ritter
Contributing editor: Daniela Kumor
French translation: Francine Rey
Contributing editor: Michèle Schreyer

For Hulton Getty:
Art director: Michael Rand
Design: Ian Denning
Managing editor: Annabel Else
Picture editor: Ali Khoja
Picture research: Alex Linghorn
Editor: James Hughes
Proof reader: Elisabeth Ihre
Scanning: Paul Wright
Production: Robert Gray
Special thanks: Leon Meyer,
Téa Aganovic and Antonia Hille

Typesetting by Greiner & Reichel Fotosatz. Colour separation by R&B Creative Services Group
Printed and bound by Sing Cheong Printing Co. Ltd., Hong Kong, China

ISBN 3-8290-0520-2

Frontispiece: 'Fascism is a religion; the twentieth century will be
known in history as the century of Fascism', Benito Mussolini.
A very young Fascist proudly salutes Il Duce at a rally in Rome, 1932.

Frontispiz: „Der Faschismus ist eine Religion, und das zwanzigste
Jahrhundert wird als das Jahrhundert des Faschismus in die Geschichte
eingehen", Benito Mussolini. Ein junger Faschist begrüßt stolz den
Duce auf einer Massenkundgebung in Rom, 1932.

Frontispice: « Le fascisme est une religion; l'histoire retiendra que le
20e siècle fut le siècle du fascisme», Benito Mussolini. Un très jeune
fasciste salue fièrement le Duce lors d'un rassemblement à Rome, 1932.

Contents / Inhalt / Sommaire

Introduction

After the wild and weird, joyriding Roaring Twenties, life came down to earth with a bump in the Thirties. As Noel Coward had predicted in his song 'Poor Little Rich Girl', it was a case of 'Cocktails and laughter, but what comes after...?' The capitalist West was hit by the worst depression it had ever known, while the communist East struggled to meet the demands it was imposing on itself through a series of five-year plans. South of the equator, it was very much business as usual: unrest in India, exploitation in South Africa, revolutions in South America. The Japanese Empire flexed its military muscles at the expense of Manchuria and China. The British Empire soldiered on, deceiving itself with delusions of permanency.

The bitterest of civil wars gave Spain a foretaste of what fascism was to serve most of Europe in the Forties. The cruel and clumsy General Franco began his purge of democracy, driving progressives, republicans, the International Brigade and Picasso from the Peninsula. Meanwhile, in Abyssinia, an Italian army equipped with poison gas and all the refinements of modern war crushed tribesmen who believed their emperor was God. In China, the Last Emperor was installed as puppet ruler by the Japanese, and six months later Mao and his followers began the Long March.

In the United States, biggest was best, except in the case of unemployment figures, which reached over eight million in 1931. Americans marvelled at the Empire State Building, Radio City Music Hall and Rockefeller Center, the Golden Gate Bridge and the Tennessee Valley Authority. Homesteaders from the Dust Bowl, driven from their farms by natural and financial disaster, drove their overloaded Model Ts to the promised land of California. Hobos hopped from one freight car to another in search of non-existent jobs. President Roosevelt promised, and at last delivered, a New Deal.

In a world which had just started to shrink, the times were good for some. It was the last great age of the shipping line and the railway company – the first great age of air travel. There was a new plaything called 'television', and the Hollywood system was in full and glorious production. Somehow or other, performers like Fred Astaire and Ginger Rogers, Benny Goodman and his clarinet, pianist Fats Waller and his mountainous humour, made people forget the mess they were in, if only for a moment.

Like in any other decade, there were heroes and villains. Those who were adored included film stars like Jean Harlow, Greta Garbo and Marlene Dietrich. Others, such as Indian politician Mohandas Gandhi, English fascist Oswald Mosley, and Mrs Wallis Simpson, for whom the British monarch gave up his throne, were seen as heroes by some, villains by others. And there were those who were picked out to be victims, with the first sinister moves against the Jews in Central Europe.

Englishman John Cobb smashed the world land speed record. In Australia, cricketer Douglas Jardine's use of 'bodyline' bowling almost smashed relations between England and that country. In America, the German-built *Hindenburg* smashed into its mooring tower in New Jersey and ended the airship age.

But at least it was still possible to get a decent domestic servant.

Einführung

Nach den wilden und unkonventionellen zwanziger Jahren landete man im folgenden Jahrzehnt recht unsanft wieder auf dem Boden der Tatsachen. Wie Noel Coward es in ihrem Lied „Armes, kleines, reiches Mädchen" prophezeite, war alles nur „Cocktail und Gelächter, aber was sollte danach kommen?" Den kapitalistischen Westen traf die schwerste Wirtschaftskrise, die er je verkraften mußte, während der kommunistische Osten verzweifelt versuchte, die selbstauferlegten Anforderungen der Fünfjahrespläne zu erfüllen. Südlich des Äquators hielt man sich weiterhin an die allgemeine Tagesordnung: Unruhen in Indien, Ausbeutung in Südafrika und Revolutionen in Südamerika. Japan besetzte die Mandschurei und begann von dort aus den Krieg gegen China. Unterdessen hielt das britische Imperium unermüdlich an der Illusion fest, daß sein Weltreich Bestand haben würde.

Der Spanische Bürgerkrieg vermittelte einen bitteren Vorgeschmack dessen, was der Faschismus in den vierziger Jahren dem größten Teil Europas antun sollte. Erbarmungslos unterdrückte General Franco jegliche Demokratiebestrebungen auf der spanischen Halbinsel, indem er Progressive, Republikaner, die Internationale Brigade und Künstler wie Picasso ins Exil trieb. Unterdessen marschierten italienische Truppen in Abessinien, dem heutigen Äthiopien, ein und überwanden, sogar unter Einsatz von Giftgas, den erbitterten Widerstand der Bevölkerung. In China setzten die Japaner den Letzten Kaiser als Marionettenherrscher ein, doch bereits ein halbes Jahr später brach Mao Tse-tung mit seinen Anhängern zum Langen Marsch in eine kommunistische Zukunft auf.

In den Vereinigten Staaten galt die Devise: je größer desto besser – mit einer Ausnahme, der Zahl der Arbeitslosen, die 1931 sogar die Acht-Millionen-Grenze überstieg. Stolz bewunderten die Amerikaner das Empire State Building, die Radio City Music Hall, das Rockefeller Center, die Golden Gate Bridge und auch die Verwaltung des Tennessee Valley.

Siedler aus den amerikanischen Trockengebieten ließen Naturkatastrophen und finanziellen Ruin hinter sich und fuhren mit ihren überladenen Model T-Autos ins gelobte Land Kalifornien. Wanderarbeiter sprangen von einem Güterwaggon zum nächsten auf der Suche nach nicht vorhandenen Arbeitsplätzen. Präsident Roosevelt versprach den New Deal und setzte dieses Programm auch in die Tat um.

Die neuen Reisemöglichkeiten relativierten die riesigen Dimensionen der Welt. Die letzte große Ära der Schiffahrtslinien und Eisenbahngesellschaften brach an, und das große Zeitalter der Flugreisen begann. Es gab ein neues Spielzeug, das sich „Fernsehen" nannte, und das Studiosystem in Hollywood produzierte einen wunderbaren Film nach dem anderen. Irgendwie gelang es Fred Astaire und Ginger Rogers, Benny Goodman und seiner Klarinette sowie Fats Waller und seinem unverwüstlichen Humor, die Menschen – wenn auch nur für einen kurzen Moment – in eine andere, sorglose Welt zu entführen.

Wie in jedem Jahrzehnt gab es auch in den dreißiger Jahren Helden und Schurken. Allgemein bewundert wurden Filmstars wie Jean Harlow, Greta Garbo und Marlene Dietrich. An manchen Persönlichkeiten schieden sich die Geister, an dem indischen Politiker Mahatma Gandhi, dem englischen Faschisten Oswald Mosley und der Amerikanerin Wallis Simpson, um derentwillen der britische Monarch abdankte. Und dann gab es noch die Opfer, als die ersten unheilverkündenden Schritte gegen die Juden in Mitteleuropa eingeleitet wurden.

Der Engländer John Cobb brach mit seinem Wagen den Geschwindigkeitsrekord. In Australien zerbrachen beinahe an Kricketspieler Douglas Jardine und seinen „Gesten" eines Bowlingspielers die anglo-australischen Beziehungen. In New Jersey ging die *Hindenburg* in Flammen auf, und beendete auf diese Weise die große Ära der Luftschiffahrt.

Doch zumindest war es damals noch möglich, gutes Hauspersonal zu finden.

Introduction

Après les années vingt qui furent aussi folles qu'extraordinaires et démesurées, la réalité fit à nouveau surface dans les années trente, non sans heurts. Noel Coward l'avait prédit dans sa chanson « Pauvre petite fille riche », tout est « cocktails et rires, mais qu'adviendra-t-il après ? » A l'Ouest, la société capitaliste fut frappée de plein fouet par la plus grave crise qu'elle ait jamais connue tandis qu'à l'Est le régime communiste s'efforçait de faire face aux exigences d'une série de plans quinquennaux qu'il avait mis en place. Au sud de l'Equateur, la situation n'évoluait guère : troubles en Inde, exploitation en Afrique du Sud, révolutions en Amérique du Sud. L'Empire japonais déployait ses forces militaires aux dépens de la Mandchourie et de la Chine et l'Empire britannique persévérait envers et contre tout, entretenant ses illusions sur la permanence des choses.

La plus sanglante des guerres civiles donna à l'Espagne un avant-goût de ce que le fascisme imposerait à l'Europe dans les années quarante. Le général Franco, cruel et brutal, entreprit sa purge antidémocratique, chassant hors de la Péninsule les forces progressistes, les républicains, les brigades internationales et Picasso. Pendant ce temps, en Abyssinie, l'armée italienne, dotée de gaz asphyxiant et d'un équipement militaire moderne et sophistiqué, écrasait les hommes d'un peuple qui vénérait son empereur comme un dieu. En Chine, le dernier empereur ne fut qu'une marionnette installée au pouvoir par les Japonais et, six mois plus tard, Mao et ses partisans entamaient leur Longue Marche.

Aux Etats-Unis, plus c'était grand, mieux c'était, à l'exception du nombre de chômeurs qui dépassait les huit millions en 1931. Les Américains s'émerveillaient devant l'Empire State Building, le music-hall de Radio City et le centre Rockefeller, le pont du Golden Gate et le programme d'emménagement de la vallée du Tennessee. Chassés de leurs terres par des désastres naturels et économiques, les fermiers du Middle West prenaient la route de la

Californie, nouvelle terre promise, au volant de leurs Fords surchargées. Les travailleurs saisonniers sautaient d'un wagon de marchandises à l'autre à la recherche d'emplois inexistants. Le président Roosevelt promit un New Deal et passa enfin à l'acte.

Dans un monde où les distances commençaient à se réduire, l'époque allait profiter à quelques-uns. La fin de l'ère des compagnies maritimes et ferroviaires marqua les grands débuts du transport aérien. Un nouveau jouet appelé « télévision » fit son apparition tandis que la machine hollywoodienne produisait un film à succès après l'autre. A leur manière, des artistes comme Fred Astaire et Ginger Rogers, Benny Goodman avec sa clarinette ou le pianiste Fats Waller débordant d'humour permirent aux gens d'oublier le désordre qui les entourait, ne serait-ce qu'un moment.

Cette décennie, comme les précédentes, connut ses héros et ses traîtres. Il y eut ceux que l'on adora, comme les stars de cinéma telles que Jean Harlow, Greta Garbo et Marlene Dietrich, et ceux qui furent des héros pour certains et des traîtres pour d'autres, comme l'homme politique indien Mahatma Gandhi, le fasciste anglais Oswald Mosley ou Wallis Simpson, pour qui le roi d'Angleterre abdiqua. Enfin, il y eut ceux qui seraient désignés comme victimes et les juifs d'Europe centrale furent les premiers à en subir les sinistres mesures.

En Angleterre, John Cobb battit le record du monde de vitesse automobile. En Australie, le joueur de cricket Douglas Jardine, employant une « gestuelle » de joueur de boules, manqua de créer un incident diplomatique entre l'Angleterre et son pays. Aux Etats-Unis, le zeppelin allemand *Hindenburg* s'écrasa contre sa tour d'attache à New Jersey, mettant ainsi un terme à l'ère du dirigeable.

Mais, Dieu merci, il était encore possible de trouver des domestiques de confiance.

1. Earning a living
Lebensunterhalt
Gagner sa vie

A street corner in Wigan, 1939. 'The total population of Wigan is a little under 87,000… at any moment more than one person in three is either drawing or living on the dole' – George Orwell, *The Road to Wigan Pier*.

An einer Straßenecke in Wigan, 1939. „Die Einwohnerzahl von Wigan liegt bei knapp 87.000… und zu jedem beliebigen Zeitpunkt beträgt der Anteil der Einwohner, die entweder Arbeitslosenunterstützung beziehen oder davon leben, über ein Drittel", schrieb George Orwell in *Der Weg nach Wigan Pier*.

Au coin d'une rue à Wigan, 1939. « La population de Wigan compte un peu moins de 87 000 habitants … à tout instant, il y a plus d'une personne sur trois qui est au chômage ou qui en vit », George Orwell, *La Route qui mène au quai Wigan*.

1. Earning a living
Lebensunterhalt
Gagner sa vie

'Oh, God, send me some work!' – Walter Greenwood, *Love on the Dole*, 1933.

Those who had work swarmed through the gates of factory and foundry, mine and mill. Those without work clustered on street corners, cloth-capped and mufflered against the cold wind of Depression. Dreams died in the labour exchange and the dole queue. The means test pared living standards down to the barebone minimum.

Men, women and whole families trudged the length and breadth of their homeland, begging for employment. Sometimes they found a few days labour, fruit-picking or other seasonal work. A permanent job remained a dream for most. If you had friends in the right place, you might become a postman or a bus driver. For women, there was domestic service or work in the light industries that were springing up along the new arterial roads.

In the United States, Roosevelt called for a New Deal, a programme of public works that would provide work for millions. In Europe, sooner or later, things began to change. Factories and shipyards reopened. Jobs became available. It seemed that better times lay ahead.

But most of the jobs were created by the race for rearmament, and the better times turned out to be World War II.

„O Gott, bitte gib mir Arbeit!" – Walter Greenwood, *Love on the Dole*, 1933.

Die Menschen, die noch Arbeit hatten, strömten in Fabriken und Gießereien, in Kohlen-gruben und Mühlen. Die Arbeitslosen versammelten sich unterdessen an Straßenecken und schützten sich mit Schlägermützen und warmen Schals gegen den kalten Wind der Wirtschafts-krise. Während sie vor dem Arbeitsamt anstanden oder auf ihre Arbeitslosenunterstützung warteten, gaben viele von ihnen ihre Träume auf. Die Berechnungsgrundlage der finanziellen Unterstützung reduzierte den Lebensstandard der Arbeitslosen auf ein absolutes Minimum.

Männer, Frauen und sogar ganze Familien zogen durch ihr Heimatland auf der Suche nach Arbeit. Gelegentlich konnten sie bei der Ernte oder anderen saisongebundenen Tätigkeiten ein paar Tage lang aushelfen. Ein fester Arbeitsplatz blieb jedoch für die meisten Suchenden lediglich ein Hoffnungsschimmer. Mit Beziehungen konnte man als Postbote oder Busfahrer arbeiten. Frauen fanden Arbeit als Hausangestellte oder auch als Fabrikarbeiterinnen in der Leichtindustrie, die sich entlang der neuen Fernverkehrsstraßen entwickelte.

In den Vereinigten Staaten versprach Roosevelt der Bevölkerung den „New Deal" – ein Programm zur Wiederbelebung der Wirtschaft. Auch in Europa begann sich langsam die Arbeitslage zu ändern. Fabriken und Schiffswerften schrieben neue Stellen aus. Es schien, als stünden bessere Zeiten bevor.

Doch die meisten neuen Arbeitsplätze waren Teil der Rüstungsindustrie – und die „besseren Zeiten" entpuppten sich schließlich als der Zweite Weltkrieg.

« Dieu, faites que je trouve du travail! », Walter Greenwood in *Love on the Dole*, 1933.

Ceux qui avaient un emploi se pressaient aux portes des usines et des fonderies, des mines et des aciéries. Ceux qui n'en avaient pas se regroupaient au coin des rues, emmitouflés dans leur cache-nez pour se protéger du vent glacial de la crise. Les rêves s'évanouissaient à la Bourse de l'emploi et dans les files de chômeurs tandis que les allocations réduisaient le niveau de vie au plus strict minimum.

Des hommes, des femmes, des familles entières arpentaient leur région, implorant pour qu'on leur donne du travail. Parfois, ils en trouvaient pour quelques jours, le temps d'une cueillette de fruits ou autre. Pour la plupart, un emploi durable ne restait qu'un rêve. Si vous aviez des amis bien placés, vous pouviez devenir postier ou conducteur de bus. Les femmes pouvaient travailler comme domestique ou dans les usines de lampes qui s'élevaient le long des nouvelles grandes routes.

Aux Etats-Unis, Roosevelt lança le « New Deal », un programme de travaux publics qui devait procurer du travail à des millions de gens. En Europe, les choses changèrent peu à peu. Les usines et les chantiers navals ouvraient à nouveau. Il y avait du travail. L'avenir semblait à nouveau sourire.

Cependant la plupart des emplois furent créés par la course au réarmement et il n'y eut pas de « jours meilleurs » mais la Seconde Guerre mondiale.

Working for the British Empire, May 1938. Men
at the Cardiff Institute weave the huge baskets that
will be used to bring oil cake from South Africa.

Arbeiten für das britische Empire, Mai 1938.
Angestellte des Cardiff-Instituts flechten riesige
Körbe, in denen Ölkuchen aus Südafrika nach
Großbritannien transportiert werden sollen.

Au service de l'Empire britannique, mai 1938.
Des ouvriers de l'Institut de Cardiff tissent
d'énormes paniers destinés au transport de
tourteaux en provenance d'Afrique du Sud.

Making the trains run to time – an obsession of
the 1930s. Staff working for the Great Western
Railway overhaul signal-box and station clocks in
the company workshops at Reading, 1934.

Die genaue Einhaltung der Fahrpläne entwickelte
sich in den dreißiger Jahren zur Leidenschaft.
Angestellte der Great Western Eisenbahngesellschaft überholen Stellwerks- und Bahnhofs-
uhren in ihren Werkstätten in Reading, 1934.

Trains à l'heure ! Une obsession des années trente.
Des employés d'une compagnie de chemins de fer
anglaise révisent les postes d'aiguillage et les
horloges des gares à Reading, 1934.

Health and safety at work, 1937 style. Men wear protective masks as they burr and sand dartboards.

Gesundheit und Sicherheit am Arbeitsplatz im Stil von 1937. Arbeiter tragen Schutzmasken bei der Bearbeitung von Dartscheiben.

Hygiène et sécurité au travail, style de 1937. Des ouvriers portent des masques protecteurs durant le rabotage et le ponçage des cibles.

The English straw hat. Mr Burns continues a 100-year-old family
tradition, making and supplying 'boaters' for the boys of Harrow School.
He was the grandson of the hat's original designer, Mrs Chatham.

Der englische Strohhut. Mr. Burns stellt „Boaters" für die Schüler der
Privatschule in Harrow her und folgt damit einer hundertjährigen
Familientradition. Seine Großmutter, Mrs. Chatham, entwarf diese
Kopfbedeckung.

Le chapeau de paille anglais. Perpétuant une tradition familiale
centenaire, M. Burns confectionne les « canotiers » destinés aux élèves de
l'école de Harrow. Il était le petit-fils de Mme Chatham, la styliste qui
créa le chapeau.

Massacre in Chicago, 1930. Hog carcasses line the walls of a meat-
packing plant. Chicago was the centre of the United States meat industry,
its enormous stockyards having been developed by the Armour family.

Massaker in Chicago, 1930. Schweinerümpfe hängen in Reih und
Glied in einem Fleischabpackbetrieb. Chicago, das seine gewaltigen
Schlachthöfe der Familie Armour verdankte, war das Zentrum der
amerikanischen Fleischindustrie.

Massacre à Chicago, 1930. Carcasses de porc alignées dans une usine
d'emballage de viande. Chicago était, aux Etats-Unis, la capitale de
l'industrie de la viande, ses énormes parcs à bestiaux avaient été
construits par la famille Armour.

Preparing for the harvest from the sea, 1937. Piles of barrels are stacked, ready for the herring season on the east coast of England. In the Thirties, there were no such things as 'fish quotas'. Fishermen took everything they could get from the sea.

Letzte Vorbereitungen für die Ernte der Meeresfrüchte, 1937. Für die Herings-saison an der Ostküste Englands werden Fässer gestapelt. In den dreißiger Jahren gab es im Fischereiwesen noch keine „Fangquoten", und Fischer fingen alles, was das Meer hergab.

Préparatifs pour la pêche en mer, 1937. Des milliers de caques sont empilées en vue de la saison des harengs sur la côte Est de l'Angleterre. Dans les années trente, les « quotas » n'existaient pas et les pêcheurs ramenaient tout ce qu'ils pouvaient pêcher.

Women assemble 'lifeboat' collection boxes for the Royal National Lifeboat Institution, November 1933. Then as now, the British lifeboat service was financed solely by voluntary contributions.

Frauen basteln Sammelbüchsen in Form von Rettungsbooten für die Royal National Lifeboat Institution, November 1933. Auch heute noch wird der britische Seenotdienst ausschließlich aus freiwilligen Spenden finanziert.

Des femmes assemblent des canots de sauvetage miniature pour la Société Royale du Sauvetage, novembre 1933. Les sauveteurs britanniques étaient et sont encore uniquement financés par des dons.

A sight that would have delighted Henry Ford. Workers check the quality of toy cars at a factory in Walthamstow, London. As men lost their jobs in the ailing heavy industries, more and more women found employment in factories like these.

Henry Ford hätte dieser Anblick gefallen. Arbeiterinnen prüfen Spielzeugautos auf ihre Qualität in einer Fabrik in Walthamstow, London. Immer mehr Frauen fanden in der Leichtindustrie Arbeit, während Männer ihre Anstellungen in der angeschlagenen Schwerindustrie verloren.

Cette scène aurait enchanté Henry Ford. Des ouvrières contrôlent la qualité des jouets à l'usine de Walthamstow, Londres. Les hommes perdaient leurs emplois dans l'industrie lourde en déclin tandis que de plus en plus de femmes étaient embauchées dans des usines comme celle-ci.

The herring arrive in Great Yarmouth, England, September 1930. The 'herring girls', who gutted, cleaned and packed the fish, worked long hours on the windswept quayside.

Eintreffen der Heringe in Great Yarmouth, England, September 1930. Die „Heringsmädchen", die die Fische ausnahmen, reinigten und verpackten, waren an ihrem langen Arbeitstag auf dem Kai Wind und Wetter ausgesetzt.

Arrivage de harengs à Great Yarmouth, Angleterre, septembre 1930. Les « filles à hareng », qui vidaient, nettoyaient et emballaient le poisson, travaillaient de longues heures sur le quai balayé par les vents.

In a sunnier clime, young boys
bring out great piles of pasta to
dry in the Italian sunshine, 1930.

Im freundlicheren Klima Italiens
trocknen große Mengen von
Pasta in der Sonne, 1930.

Climat plus clément. De jeunes
garçons sortent des piles de
pâtes pour les faire sécher sous
le soleil d'Italie, 1930.

A Welsh chain gang.
Men work with
hammers and files
to make heavy-duty
chains at a steel
foundry in
Pontypridd, March
1937.

Eine walisische
Kettenreaktion.
Männer arbeiten mit
Hämmern und
Feilen an schweren
Ketten in einer
Stahlgießerei in
Pontypridd, März
1937.

Les maillons de la
chaîne, mars 1397.
Des ouvriers
travaillent au
marteau et à la lime
la finition des
chaînes fabriquées
dans une aciérie de
Pontypridd, Pays de
Galles.

Clog-makers in a London factory, 1932. Many working-class factory hands still preferred clogs, which were hard-wearing and protected the feet far better than ordinary shoes.

Holzschuhmacher in einer Londoner Fabrik, 1932. Viele Angehörige der Arbeiterklasse trugen am liebsten Clogs, weil sie strapazierfähig waren und die Füße bei der Fabrikarbeit weit besser schützten als normale Schuhe.

Sabotières dans une usine de Londres, 1932. Bien des ouvriers qui travaillaient en usine préféraient encore porter des sabots qui étaient solides et protégeaient mieux leurs pieds que les chaussures ordinaires.

Workmen put the finishing
touches to a high-pressure
steam boiler for the Shipping,
Engineering and Machinery
exhibition at Olympia, London,
in September 1933. Shows
such as this were intended to
raise the morale of workers
who feared that the end of
one job could mean the end of
work entirely.

Arbeiter geben einem
Hochdruckdampfkessel den
letzten Schliff für eine
Schiffahrts-, Konstruktions- und
Maschinenschau in Olympia,
London, September 1933.
Solche Ausstellungen sollten
Arbeitern moralischen Auftrieb
geben, die befürchteten, nie
wieder Arbeit zu finden, wenn
sie ihren Job verlieren.

Derniers réglages d'un moteur
à vapeur à haute pression au
Salon de la navigation, de
l'ingénierie et de la machinerie
à l'Olympia, Londres, septembre
1933. De telles expositions
étaient censées remonter
le moral des travailleurs qui
craignaient de ne jamais
retrouver du travail s'ils
perdaient leur emploi.

Assembling oil stoves in a Birmingham factory, 1931.
It was in this year that thousands of unemployed in Europe
and the United States took to the streets and rioted.

Montage von Ölöfen in einer Fabrik in Birmingham,
1931. In diesem Jahr zogen Tausende von Europäern
und Amerikanern durch die Straßen, um gegen die
Arbeitslosigkeit zu demonstrieren.

Assemblage de poêles à mazout dans une usine de
Birmingham, 1931. Cette année-là des milliers de
chômeurs en Europe et aux Etats-Unis descendirent
dans la rue et se livrèrent à de violentes bagarres.

February 1930. The first great age of family motoring. Workmen
on the production line at Morris Motors in Cowley, Oxford, rub
down the car's bodywork in between coats of paint.

Februar 1930. In den dreißiger Jahren wird das Auto zum
Familienfahrzeug. Arbeiter an der Fertigungsstraße von Morris
Motors in Cowley, Oxford, reinigen die Karosserien zwischen
den einzelnen Lackierungen.

Février 1930. La première grande période de l'automobile
familiale. Des ouvriers sur une chaîne de production Morris
Motors à Cowley, Oxford, astiquent la carrosserie d'une voiture
entre deux couches de peinture.

A British sailor
paints the cable of
HMS *Thruster* in
the port of
Alexandria, Egypt,
February 1936.

Ein britischer
Matrose streicht die
Ankerkette der
HMS *Thruster* im
Hafen von
Alexandria, Ägypten,
Februar 1936.

Un marin
britannique peint
l'amarre du navire
HMS *Thruster* dans
le port d'Alexandrie,
Egypte, février
1936.

Men working at the Craig-Ddu slate quarry in Merionethshire, Wales, January 1934. The men have finished their shift and are about to roll down the valley to their homes on trolleys known as *car-gwyllts* ('the car that goes').

Arbeiter des walisischen Craig-Ddu Schieferbruchs in Merionethshire im Januar 1934. Die Männer haben ihre Schicht beendet und sind im Begriff, auf einem „car-gwyllt" („der Wagen, der von selbst fährt") ins Tal hinunterzurollen.

Ouvriers de la carrière d'ardoise de Craig-Ddu à Merionethshire, Pays de Galles, janvier 1934. Ils ont terminé leur journée et s'apprêtent à rentrer chez eux en bas dans la vallée, assis sur ce chariot surnommé la « voiture qui roule toute seule ».

Mexborough, Yorkshire, 1935. Young coalminers
learn how to harness and handle pit ponies
deep underground at the Manvers main colliery.

Mexborough, Yorkshire, 1935. In der
Hauptzeche der Stadt Manvers lernen junge
Bergleute tief unter der Erde, wie man Gruben-
ponys anschirrt und führt.

Mexborough, Yorkshire, 1935. De jeunes
mineurs apprennent à harnacher et conduire les
chevaux de mine au fond de la galerie principale
de Manvers.

Trainee miners at a colliery school in Ashington, County Durham, 1939. 'If a miner's working life is 40 years the chances are nearly 7 to 1 against his escaping injury and not much more than 20 to 1 against his being killed outright' – George Orwell, *The Road to Wigan Pier*.

Bergarbeiter-Lehrlinge in einer Grubenschule in Ashington, Grafschaft Durham, 1939. „Wenn das Arbeitsleben eines Bergmannes 40 Jahre beträgt, stehen die Chancen fast 7 zu 1, daß er verletzt wird, und nicht viel besser als 20 zu 1, daß er auf der Stelle getötet wird", schrieb George Orwell in *Der Weg nach Wigan Pier*.

Apprentis-mineurs à l'école des mines de Ashington, comté de Durham, 1939. « Comptant qu'un mineur travaille quarante ans, il y a à peu près une chance sur sept qu'il soit blessé et plus d'une chance sur vingt qu'il soit tué sur le coup » – George Orwell, *La Route qui mène au quai Wigan*.

Carriage and wagon wheels in
a railway factory, 1935. Across the
whole world, railways were the
backbone of every transport
system. They carried almost all
overland freight.

Wagen- und Waggonräder in einer
Eisenbahnfabrik, 1935. Überall auf
der Welt bildeten die Eisenbahnen
das Rückgrat der Transportsysteme
und beförderten nahezu sämtliche
auf dem Landweg verschickten
Frachtgüter.

Roues de wagons dans une usine
des chemins de fer, 1935. Partout
dans le monde, le train constituait
le nerf des réseaux de transports et
assurait presque la totalité du
transport de marchandises par voie
de terre.

Slum clearance, London 1931. Demolition workers bring down
condemned houses in Paddington. Such work was physically
tough, dangerous, and unpleasant. The slums that they
destroyed were infested with rats, lice and other vermin.

Abriß der Slums, London, 1931. Arbeiter demolieren zum
Abbruch bestimmte Häuser im Stadtteil Paddington. Diese
Arbeit war hart, gefährlich und unangenehm, denn die Slums
waren mit Ratten, Läusen und anderem Ungeziefer verseucht.

Destruction d'un taudis, Londres, 1931. A Paddington, des
ouvriers démolissent des maisons condamnées. Un tel travail
était dur, dangereux et rébarbatif, les taudis étant infestés de
rats, de poux et autre vermine.

Men burn effigies of
vermin to celebrate
the destruction of
slums in Sidney
Street and
Clarendon Street in
the London borough
of St Pancras.

Arbeiter verbrennen
Nachbildungen von
Schädlingen, um den
Abriß der Slums im
Bereich Sidney Street
und Clarendon
Street im Londoner
Stadtteil St. Pancras
zu feiern.

Des ouvriers brûlent
des effigies de
vermine pour
célébrer la
démolition des
taudis de Sidney
Street et de
Clarendon Street à
St. Pancras, un
arrondissement de
Londres.

London shoeshine, July 1934. A workman polishes part of the massive Quadriga (four-horsed chariot) bronze statue at Constitution Arch, Hyde Park Corner. Shortly before the statue was finished, Lord Michelham, financier of the project, gave a dinner party for eight people inside one of the horses.

Londoner Schuhputzdienst, Juli 1934. Ein Arbeiter poliert einen Pferdehuf des vierspännigen bronzenen Streitwagens auf dem Constitution Arch am Hyde Park Corner. Kurz vor Fertigstellung der Quadriga lud der Finanzier des Projekts, Lord Michelham, acht Personen zu einer Abendgesellschaft im Inneren eines der Pferde ein.

Londres resplendit, juillet 1934. Un ouvrier polit le sabot d'un des chevaux du quadrige en bronze sur l'Arc de la Constitution, Hyde Park Corner. La statue n'était pas encore terminée quand Lord Michelham, mécène du projet, donna un dîner pour huit personnes à l'intérieur de l'un des chevaux.

The unusually shaped rudder of the SS *Arctees*, designed by Sir Joseph Isherwood and launched at Haverton-on-Tees, County Durham, 1934.

Das ungewöhnlich geformte Ruder der von Sir Joseph Isherwood entworfenen SS *Arctees*, die in Haverton-on-Tees in der Grafschaft Durham 1934 vom Stapel gelassen wurde.

Gouvernail de forme inhabituelle pour le navire SS *Arctees*, conçu par Sir Joseph Isherwood et mis à la mer à Haverton-on-Tees, comté de Durham, 1934.

The Manhattan skyline comes of age in the 1930s. Here, steelworkers take a break to admire the city. They are standing on scaffolding at the very top of the 70-storey RCA building in the Rockefeller Center, New York, December 1934.

Die Skyline von Manhattan entwickelt in den dreißiger Jahren ihr charakteristisches Bild. Stahlarbeiter bewundern während einer Pause die Stadt. Das Gerüst, auf dem sie stehen, befindet sich auf der Spitze des 70stöckigen RCA-Gebäudes im New Yorker Rockefeller Center, Dezember 1934.

Le panorama de Manhattan s'affirme dans les années trente. Des métallurgistes font une pause pour admirer la ville, debout sur un échafaudage au sommet d'un gratte-ciel de 70 étages du Rockefeller Center, New York, décembre 1934.

October 1937.
Electricians install
lights on the Eiffel
Tower to illuminate
the city during the
Paris Exhibition.

Oktober 1937.
Elektriker bringen
Scheinwerfer auf
dem Eiffelturm an,
um die Stadt
während der Pariser
Ausstellung in
festlichem Glanz
erstrahlen zu lassen.

Octobre 1937. Des
électriciens installent
un éclairage sur la
Tour Eiffel pour
illuminer la ville
durant l'Exposition
de Paris.

April 1936. Lines of
luxury. Agricultural
labourers place
cloches over rows of
strawberry plants
near Salisbury.

April 1936. Luxus
auf der ganzen Linie.
Landarbeiter stülpen
Schutzhauben über
junge Erdbeer-
pflanzen in der Nähe
von Salisbury.

Avril 1936. Fruits de
luxe en série. Des
ouvriers agricoles
placent des cloches
sur des rangées de
plants de fraise près
de Salisbury.

Cleaning and painting the glass roof at
York railway station, 1934. In the age of
steam locomotives, roofs such as this
quickly became covered in dust and grime.

Das Glasdach des Bahnhofs von York
wird gereinigt und frisch gestrichen, 1934.
Im Zeitalter der Dampfloks überzog
solche Dächer schon nach kurzer Zeit eine
dicke Staub- und Rußschicht.

Nettoyage et peinture de la verrière de la
gare de York, 1934. A l'époque des
locomotives à vapeur, les toits comme
ceux-ci étaient très vite recouverts de
poussière et de saleté.

Workmen carefully lift a pane of curved glass into a shop
front in Jermyn Street, London, April 1936. The sheet of
glass was over 20 feet (7 metres) long and five feet (1.75
metres) high.

Arbeiter setzen eine Scheibe aus gewölbtem Tafelglas in eine
Ladenfassade der Londoner Jermyn Street ein, April 1936.
Die Glasscheibe war sieben Meter breit und 1,75 Meter hoch.

Des ouvriers soulèvent avec précaution une plaque de verre
convexe pour entrer dans un magasin de Jermyn Street,
Londres, avril 1936. Cette plaque de verre mesurait sept
mètres de long et 1,75 mètres de haut.

Garden in the sky. A woman waters plants in the window of a typical Thirties high-rise building. For office staff, working conditions had never been better.

Ein Garten im Himmel. Grünpflanzen vor dem Fenster eines typischen Hochhauses der dreißiger Jahre. Für Büroangestellte waren die Arbeitsbedingungen so gut wie nie zuvor.

Jardin suspendu. Une femme arrose des plantes sur le rebord d'une fenêtre d'une tour caractéristique des années trente. Les conditions de travail des employés de bureau n'avaient jamais été aussi bonnes.

Masses on the munch. Employees of
the National Cash Register Company
lunch together in the immense staff
dining room, 1935.

Die Massen beim Essen. Angestellte der
National Cash Register Company beim
gemeinsamen Mittagessen in der großen
Kantine, 1935.

Les masses à table. Les employés de la
National Cash Register Company déjeunent
dans l'immense cantine du personnel, 1935.

Cannery Row. Women in a United States canning factory peel and prepare tomatoes, February 1930. In an age before freezers, canned food was the main bulk of any larder or food cupboard.

Dose an Dose. In einer amerikanischen Konservenfabrik schälen und bearbeiten Frauen Tomaten, Februar 1930. Als es noch keine Kühlschränke gab, füllte überwiegend Dosennahrung Speisekammern und Vorratsschränke.

Travail à la chaîne. Des ouvrières d'une fabrique de conserves aux Etats-Unis pèlent et coupent des tomates, février 1930. Les congélateurs n'existaient pas encore et les garde-manger étaient remplis de boîtes de conserve.

A break from work on a Soviet collective
farm – with not a commissar in sight, 1930.
Members of the farm's club relax in the
Buryat Mongolian Autonomous Republic.

Eine Arbeitspause in einer landwirtschaft-
lichen Produktionsgenossenschaft der
Sowjetunion – und kein Kommissar in Sicht,
1930. Die Genossenschaftsmitglieder
entspannen sich in der Burjätischen
Autonomen Sozialistischen Sowjetrepublik.

Repos dans une ferme collective soviétique –
pas un commissaire en vue, 1930. Détente
pour les membres d'une association agricole à
Buryat en République populaire de Mongolie.

'Herring girls' at Great Yarmouth rest in the late autumn sunshine, 1933. Although they were paid for the amount of work they did, not the time it took, moments like this were precious.

„Heringsmädchen" in Great Yarmouth genießen 1933 den spätherbstlichen Sonnenschein. Da sie nach geleisteter Arbeit und nicht nach Arbeitszeit bezahlt wurden, waren solche Augenblicke sehr kostbar.

Les « filles à harengs » de Great Yarmouth font une pause au soleil, fin de l'automne, 1933. Bien qu'on les ait payées à la pièce et non à l'heure, des moments comme celui-ci étaient précieux.

Workmen rest by the clock high up on the Midland Grand Hotel,
St Pancras, London, 1931. The clock was 270 feet (85 metres)
above street level. In the distance far below is King's Cross.

Zwei Arbeiter machen Mittagspause neben der Uhr des Midland
Grand Hotels in St. Pancras, London, 1931. Die Uhr befand
sich in 85 Metern Höhe. Im Hintergrund, weit unten, liegt
King's Cross.

Des ouvriers se reposent près de l'horloge à côté du Midland
Grand Hotel à St. Pancras, Londres, 1931. L'horloge était
à 85 mètres de hauteur. Au loin, bien plus bas, on distingue
King's Cross.

A view from the top. Workmen pause to take refreshment on the glass roof of Paddington station, London, 1930. The roof was made of four arches, with a total span of more than 300 feet (almost 100 metres).

Der Blick von oben. Einige Arbeiter nehmen auf dem Glasdach des Londoner Bahnhofs Paddington eine kleine Stärkung zu sich, 1930. Das Dach ruhte auf vier Bögen und besaß eine Spannweite von fast 100 Metern.

Vue d'en haut. Des ouvriers font une pause pour se rafraîchir sur la verrière de la gare de Paddington, Londres, 1930. Le toit était constitué de quatre arcs pour une travée totale de près de 100 mètres.

The American milk bar comes to Britain, 1937. American culture in all its forms was lapped up in Europe in the Thirties.

Die amerikanische Milchbar hält 1937 Einzug in Großbritannien. Die amerikanische Kultur war in all ihren Facetten in den dreißiger Jahren in Europa sehr beliebt.

Arrivée du milk-bar américain en Grande-Bretagne, 1937. Dans les années trente, la culture américaine sous toutes ses formes fut accueillie avec enthousiasme dans toute l'Europe.

October 1938.
A government
messenger at a New
York cable company
uses skates to
speed her message
through.

Eilzustellung in
einem New Yorker
Telegrafenamt,
Oktober 1938.
Eine Botin der
Regierung fährt auf
Rollschuhen, um
die Mitteilungen
schneller zu verteilen

Compagnie de
télécommunications
à New York,
octobre 1938.
Une messagère du
gouvernement se
déplace en patins
à roulettes pour
remettre les
télégrammes plus
rapidement.

The Central
Telegraph Office of
the GPO in London,
October 1932.
At that time it
employed 3,000
staff.

Das Zentrale
Telegrafenamt der
Londoner Haupt-
post, Oktober 1932.
Zu jener Zeit waren
dort 3.000 Ange-
stellte beschäftigt.

Bureau des
Télégrammes à la
Poste centrale à
Londres, octobre
1932. A cette
époque, 3 000
personnes y
travaillaient.

Telegraph boys line up at the Central Telegraph Office. The Office processed and dispatched over 50 million telegrams a year. Internal communication was through 12 miles (19 kilometres) of pneumatic tubes that snaked through the floors and ceilings.

Telegrammboten warten im Zentralen Telegrafenamt auf ihren Einsatz. Zur hausinternen Kommunikation benutzte man ein 19 Kilometer langes System von Druckluftrohren, die in Fußböden und Zimmerdecken verlegt waren. Das Amt bearbeitete und verschickte jährlich über 50 Millionen Telegramme.

Des messagers font la queue devant un guichet du Bureau des Télégrammes qui recevait et émettait plus de 50 millions de télégrammes par an. La distribution interne s'effectuait grâce aux 19 kilomètres de tubes pneumatiques qui traversaient les étages le long des plafonds.

The Mayor of Bethnal Green, London, November
1931. Councillor T Brooks vowed that elevation to
such high office would not go to his head, and that
he would continue to work as a chimney sweep.

Der Bürgermeister des Londoner Stadtteils Bethnal
Green, November 1931. Stadtrat T. Brooks
versprach seinen Wählern, daß sein neues Amt ihm
nicht zu Kopfe steigen werde und er auch weiterhin
seiner Arbeit als Schornsteinfeger nachgehen wolle.

Le maire de Bethnal Green, Londres, novembre
1931. L'élu T. Brooks fit le serment que sa
nomination à un poste aussi important ne lui
monterait pas à la tête et qu'il continuerait à
travailler comme ramoneur.

A lost-property office in
Britain, 1932. The
crutches had been left
on a train at Skegness
holiday resort.

Ein britisches Fundbüro,
1932. Die Krücken fand
man in einem Zug im
Ferienort Skegness.

Bureau des objets
trouvés en Grande-
Bretagne, 1932. Ces
béquilles ont été oubliées
dans un train à
destination de Skegness,
une station balnéaire.

Two views of unemployment in the Thirties. Kurt Hutton's portrait (above) of Alfred Smith and others looking for work in a labour exchange. Smith was 35 years old, had four children and had been out of work for three years. The sign (right) aims at humour, but betrays an underlying desperation. To 'know 3 trades' and 'speak 3 languages' did not guarantee a job.

Zwei Aufnahmen, die die Situation der Arbeitslosen in den dreißiger Jahren verdeutlichen. Kurt Huttons Foto (oben) zeigt Alfred Smith und andere bei der Jobsuche auf einem Arbeitsamt. Smith, 35 Jahre alt, hatte vier Kinder und war seit drei Jahren arbeitslos. Das Schild des Arbeitslosen (rechts) soll humorvoll klingen, verrät jedoch auch seine Verzweiflung. Die Tatsache „3 Branchen zu kennen" und „3 Sprachen zu sprechen" garantierte nicht unbedingt einen Job.

Deux clichés sur le chômage des années trente. Portrait (ci-dessus) par Kurt Hutton d'Alfred Smith et d'hommes cherchant un travail à la Bourse de l'emploi. Smith, 35 ans et père de quatre enfants, était au chômage depuis trois ans. La pancarte (à droite) se veut drôle mais laisse percer le désespoir. Le fait de « connaître 3 métiers » et de « parler 3 langues » n'était pas une garantie d'emploi.

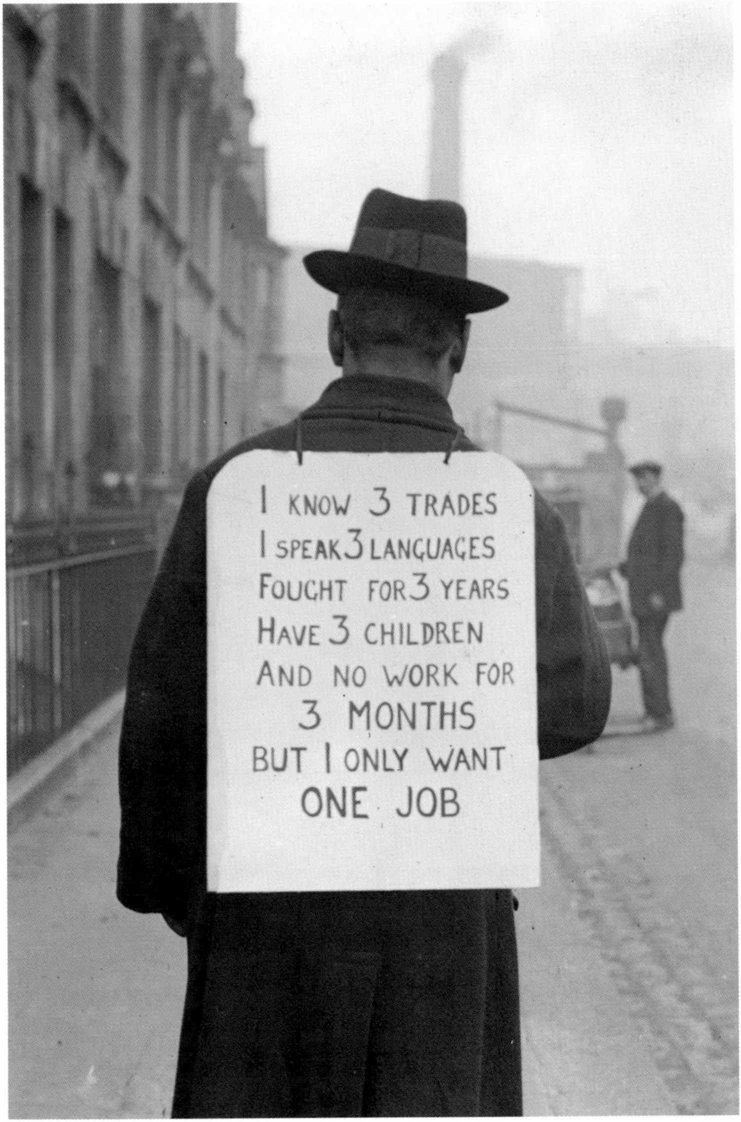
I KNOW 3 TRADES
I SPEAK 3 LANGUAGES
FOUGHT FOR 3 YEARS
HAVE 3 CHILDREN
AND NO WORK FOR
3 MONTHS
BUT I ONLY WANT
ONE JOB

London, January 1939. Police saw through a chain which a member of the National Unemployed Workers Movement has used to fasten himself to the railings of the Stepney employment exchange. He was protesting at the government's refusal to grant extra winter relief.

London, Januar 1939. Ein Polizist zersägt eine Kette, mit der sich ein Mitglied der Nationalen Bewegung Erwerbsloser Arbeiter an den Zaun des Arbeitsamtes von Stepney angekettet hat. Diese Protestaktion richtete sich gegen die Regierung, die die zusätzliche Winterhilfe abgelehnt hatte.

Londres, janvier 1939. Un policier scie la chaîne d'un manifestant du Mouvement national des chômeurs qui s'est attaché aux grilles de l'agence pour l'emploi de Stepney. Il protestait contre le refus du gouvernement d'accorder une aide supplémentaire pour l'hiver.

October 1936. The Jarrow March passes through Lavendon, near Bedford. The marchers covered nearly 300 miles (ca. 500 kilometres) in a month, from Jarrow, near Newcastle, to London, in order to highlight the appalling level of unemployment in their home town.

Oktober 1936. Der „Marsch von Jarrow" zieht durch Lavendon bei Bedford. Innerhalb eines Monats legten die Demonstranten auf dem Weg von Jarrow nach London fast 500 Kilometer zurück, um auf die erschreckend hohe Arbeitslosigkeit in ihrer Heimatstadt aufmerksam zu machen.

Octobre 1936. La Croisade de Jarrow traverse Lavendon, près de Bedford. Les manifestants marchèrent de Jarrow, près de Newcastle, jusqu'à Londres, soit près de 500 kilomètres en un mois, pour témoigner du terrifiant taux de chômage qui sévissait dans leur ville.

'I see one-third of a nation ill-housed, ill-clad,
ill-nourished' – Franklin Delano Roosevelt,
President of the United States, 1937. At that time
there were 14 million unemployed in the USA.

„Ein Drittel der Bevölkerung unserer Nation ist
mangelhaft untergebracht, mangelhaft gekleidet
und mangelhaft ernährt", sagte Franklin Delano
Roosevelt, Präsident der Vereinigten Staaten,
1937. Zu jener Zeit gab es in den USA
14 Millionen Arbeitslose.

« Je vois un tiers de la nation mal logé, mal
habillé, mal nourri », Franklin Delano Roosevelt,
président des Etats-Unis, 1937. A cette époque,
le pays comptait 14 millions de chômeurs.

Dorothea Lange's famous portrait of a migrant mother in the depths of the American Depression, 1936. Thousands of families drifted west to California, desperately looking for work.

Auf dem Höhepunkt der amerikanischen Wirtschaftskrise, 1936, fotografierte Dorothea Lange diese Wander-arbeiterin und Mutter. Auf der verzweifelten Suche nach Arbeit zogen Tausende von Familien in den Westen nach Kalifornien.

Le célèbre portrait signé Dorothea Lange d'une mère migrante au plus fort de la crise américaine, 1936. Des milliers de familles se déplacèrent vers l'Ouest, en direction de la Californie, cherchant désespérément du travail.

An American 'bum' escapes for a while from the misery of life, 1939. Three years later he may well have been smartly dressed, well fed, with the finest dental and medical treatment – but it took a war to bring about this change.

Ein amerikanischer Obdachloser entflieht für kurze Zeit dem Elend seines Lebens, 1939. Drei Jahre später war er möglicherweise gut gekleidet, wohlgenährt und erfreute sich der besten ärztlichen und zahnärztlichen Behandlung – es bedurfte allerdings eines Krieges, um diese Wende herbeizuführen.

Le temps d'une sieste, ce clochard américain oublie la misère, 1939. Trois ans plus tard, il sera certes bien habillé, bien nourri et soigné par les meilleurs médecins et dentistes – mais il aura fallu une guerre pour permettre un tel changement.

August 1936.
A photograph by
Dorothea Lange
portrays refugees
from drought-
stricken Oklahoma
sheltering at Blythe,
California.

August, 1936. Diese
Aufnahme von
Dorothea Lange
zeigt Flüchtlinge aus
dem von Dürre-
katastrophen
heimgesuchten
Oklahoma, die in
Blythe in Kalifornien
Schutz suchen.

Août 1936. Une
photo de Dorothea
Lange montre des
réfugiés dans un abri
de fortune à Blythe,
Californie, après
avoir fui l'Oklahoma
dévasté par la
sécheresse.

2. Haves and have-nots
Arm und Reich
Les nantis et les démunis

Gerti Deutsch's portrait of a Cambridge University bedmaker, 1939.
The woman's job was to clean the rooms of undergraduates, the vast ·
majority of whom came from the upper and upper-middle classes. The
bedmaker and her young gentlemen lived lives that were worlds apart.

Gerti Deutsch fotografierte ein Zimmermädchen der Universität
Cambridge, 1939. Sie reinigte die Zimmer der Studenten, die
größtenteils den gesellschaftlichen Kreisen der Oberschicht und
der oberen Mittelschicht angehörten. Zwischen dem Alltag der
Bettenmacherin und dem ihrer jungen Herren lagen Welten.

Portrait d'une femme de chambre à l'Université de Cambridge,
par Gerti Deutsch, 1939. Elle faisait le ménage dans les chambres
des étudiants pour la plupart issus de l'aristocratie ou de la haute
bourgeoisie. La femme de chambre et les jeunes gens vivaient dans
des mondes que tout séparait.

2. Haves and have-nots
Arm und Reich
Les nantis et les démunis

As the Wall Street Crash of 1929 began to take effect, the Western world reeled into the trauma of the Thirties. Everyday life was a hit-or-miss affair. If you still had a job, you could afford to roll back the carpet and quickstep to the best dance bands that popular music has ever known. The middle classes paid ever more attention to daintiness and the niceties of life. The rich did what they always had done – exactly what they wanted to do.

If you were unemployed – and tens of millions were – it didn't matter where you lived, life was hell. On street corners of every town and city in Europe, knots of unemployed gathered to seek what comfort there was in shared misery. In the heartlands of rural America, local banks went bust, dragging down with them farmers whose dust-bowl homesteads were mortgaged to the hilt.

In the Soviet Union, the bliss of post-revolutionary dawn turned to a bitter fight to meet the demands of Stalinism. The response was heroic, the reality heartbreaking.

But the cinema flourished. Instead of having babies, those who could afford to bought baby cars. Policemen dealt with young offenders by means of a cuff on the head. Murderers were executed. Had it not been for all those unemployed, life could have been very pleasant.

Als nach 1929 die Auswirkungen des „Schwarzen Freitags" an der New Yorker Börse deutlich wurden, begann für den Westen das Trauma der Weltwirtschaftskrise. Jeder Tag konnte zu einem Erfolg oder Mißerfolg werden. Wer noch Arbeit hatte, amüsierte sich bei der Musik der besten Tanzkapellen, die es je gab. Die Mittelschicht konzentrierte ihre Aufmerksamkeit zunehmend auf die schönen Dinge des Lebens, und die gehobenen Kreise widmeten sich ihrem gewohnten Lebensstil.

Für die Arbeitslosen aber war das Leben die reine Hölle – egal wo sie lebten. In allen europäischen Städten versammelten sie sich an Straßenecken, um im geteilten Leid Trost zu suchen. Im ländlichen Herzen Amerikas standen die örtlichen Banken vor dem Ruin und zogen die hochverschuldeten Farmer mit ins Elend.

In der Sowjetunion folgte auf das Hochgefühl der erfolgreichen Revolution der ernüchternde Kampf um die Erfüllung der Anforderungen des Stalinismus. Der Einsatz war nahezu heroisch, die Realität eher tragisch.

Das Kino jedoch florierte. Und wer es sich leisten konnte, schaffte sich eher einen Kleinwagen an, als daß er Kinder bekam. Polizisten wiesen jugendliche Straftäter noch mit Ohrfeigen auf den rechten Weg. Mörder mußten ihr Vergehen allerdings mit dem Leben bezahlen. Wäre die Arbeitslosigkeit nicht so hoch gewesen, hätte das Leben sehr angenehm sein können.

Les conséquences du krach de Wall Street en 1929 commençaient à se faire sentir et le monde occidental s'engagea chancelant dans l'ère trouble des années trente. Tout pouvait être remis en question du jour au lendemain. Si vous aviez toujours un emploi, vous pouviez rouler votre tapis et danser le fox-trot au son des meilleurs orchestres de musique populaire. Plus que jamais, les classes moyennes goûtaient au raffinement et aux bonnes choses de la vie. Quant aux riches, ils faisaient, comme toujours, tout ce qui leur plaisait.

Si vous étiez au chômage, et c'était le cas de dizaines de millions de gens, peu importe où vous habitiez, la vie était un enfer. À tous les coins de rue des villes et villages d'Europe, des chômeurs se regroupaient pour se réconforter, unis dans la misère. Au cœur de l'Amérique rurale, les banques locales faisaient faillite, entraînant dans leur chute les fermiers du Middle West dont les propriétés étaient sur-hypothéquées.

En Union soviétique, le bonheur des lendemains révolutionnaires fit place à une lutte âpre pour faire face aux exigences du stalinisme. La réponse fut héroïque, la réalité déchirante.

Ailleurs, le cinéma était florissant. Les gens aisés préféraient s'acheter des mini-voitures plutôt que de faire des enfants. La police réglait le compte des jeunes délinquants à coup de gifles et les assassins étaient exécutés. S'il n'y avait pas eu tous ces chômeurs, la vie aurait été très agréable.

Eton versus Harrow at Lord's Cricket ground, London, 1937. Two young toffs maintain stiff upper lips in the face of some ribald scrutiny from local children. The Eton and Harrow game was one of the highlights of the London Season.

Eton gegen Harrow auf dem Lord's Cricket Ground, London, 1937. Zwei junge Herren des Teams aus Eton bewahren britische Haltung, während einige Kinder sie kritisch taxieren. Die Kricket-Begegnung zwischen Eton und Harrow war ein Höhepunkt der Londoner Saison.

Eton contre Harrow sur le terrain de cricket des Lord's, Londres, 1937. Deux jeunes dandys impassibles face aux railleries d'enfants du quartier qui les dévisagent d'un air moqueur. Le match Eton-Harrow était l'un des grands événements de la saison londonienne.

Tickets for the stalls. Two theatre-goers hurry past
some of the Covent Garden market stalls on their
way to the Royal Opera House, London, 1939.

Eintrittskarten fürs Parkett. Zwei Theaterbesucher
eilen auf ihrem Weg ins Royal Opera House an
Obst- und Gemüseständen des Covent Garden
Market vorüber, London, 1939.

Billets pour l'orchestre. Deux habitués du théâtre
pressent le pas devant les étals du marché
de Covent Garden sur le chemin de l'Opéra
à Londres, 1939.

London's East End, October 1938. The infants in this picture of a
Whitechapel street may well have been the grandchildren of the Jewish
refugees who had settled here in the years leading up to World War I.

Das Londoner East End, Oktober 1938. Die Kleinkinder auf dieser
Aufnahme des Stadtteils Whitechapel waren vermutlich die Enkel der
jüdischen Flüchtlinge, die sich vor dem Ersten Weltkrieg hier ange-
siedelt hatten.

East End, Londres, octobre 1938. Les enfants de ce cliché pris dans
une rue de Whitechapel pourraient bien être les petits-enfants des
réfugiés juifs qui s'installèrent dans le quartier quelques années avant
la Première Guerre mondiale.

Rotten Row, Hyde Park, London, February 1930.
The infants being pushed in their prams by nannies
were almost certainly scions of long-established
English families.

Rotten Row, Hyde Park, London, Februar 1930.
Diese beiden Kindermädchen fahren wohl
Sprößlinge alteingesessener englischer Familien aus.

Rotten Row, Hyde Park, Londres, février 1930.
Ces enfants que des nurses promènent dans leurs
landaus sont sûrement les descendants de très
vieilles familles anglaises.

The rich at play. Mrs and Miss Daphne Duke and Mr Lander chat together before the start of the Mid-Surrey Draghound Meet, 1935. Despite the introduction of death duties some decades earlier, social life in rural areas went on virtually unchanged.

Die Reichen und ihre Vergnügungen. Mrs. und Miss Daphne Duke mit Mr. Lander auf einer Jagdgesellschaft in Mid-Surrey, 1935. Obwohl die Regierung einige Jahrzehnte zuvor die Erbschaftssteuer eingeführt hatte, wurde das gesellschaftliche Leben auf dem Lande hierdurch kaum beeinträchtigt.

Les riches s'amusent. Mme et Mlle Daphne Duke bavardent avec M. Lander avant le début d'une chasse à courre dans le Mid-Surrey, 1935. Malgré l'instauration des droits de succession quelques décennies plus tôt, la vie sociale en milieu rural suivait son cours, presque inchangée.

The poor at play. Two young boys play
'tin can golf' on a strip of waste land.

Die Armen und ihre Vergnügungen.
Zwei Jungen beim „Blechdosengolf"
auf einem Streifen Ödland.

Les pauvres s'amusent. Deux garçons
jouent au « mini-golf » sur un chemin
dans un terrain vague.

A snack bar in the Lambeth Walk, London, December 1938. The street had become famous a year earlier when it was the title of a hit number in the musical show *Me and My Gal*. American-style snack bars became increasingly popular in the Thirties.

Eine Imbißstube auf dem Londoner Lambeth Walk, Dezember 1938. Diese Straße war ein Jahr zuvor durch das gleichnamige Lied aus dem Musical *Me and My Gal* berühmt geworden. Snack-Bars im amerikanischen Stil erlangten in den dreißiger Jahren hohe Beliebtheit.

Snack-bar sur Lambeth Walk, Londres, décembre 1938. Cette rue était devenue célèbre un an plus tôt parce qu'elle était la chanson-titre de la comédie musicale intitulée *Me and My Gal*. Les snack-bars à l'américaine devinrent très populaires dans les années trente.

A Piccadilly Circus milk bar, October 1938, photographed by
Kurt Hutton. Milk bars were introduced to London by Charles Forte,
who later became a multi-millionaire hotel and restaurant owner.

Eine Milchbar am Piccadilly Circus, Oktober 1938, fotografiert von
Kurt Hutton. Charles Forte, der die amerikanische Milchbar in
London eingeführt hatte, wurde später millionenschwerer Hotel- und
Restaurantbesitzer.

Milk-bar à Piccadilly Circus, octobre 1938, photographié par
Kurt Hutton. Les milk-bars furent créés à Londres par Charles Forte
qui allait devenir un propriétaire d'hôtels et de restaurants
multimillionnaire.

'Any evening, any day, when you're walking Lambeth way, you'll find us all,
doing the Lambeth Walk…' Miss Dipper and Billy Pearce, the Peanut and
Toffee King, perform their version of the dance from the West End musical.

„Jeden Abend, jeden Tag, wer nach Lambeth kommen mag, findet uns alle
dort, und wir tanzen den 'Lambeth Walk' …" Erdnuß- und Toffeekönig
Billy Pearce und Miss Dipper führen ihre eigene Version des Tanzes aus
dem West-End-Musical vor.

« Tous les soirs, tous les jours, si vous vous promenez par Lambeth, vous
nous trouverez tous, marchant et chantant à la mode de Lambeth… » Miss
Dipper et Billy Pearce, le roi du caramel à la cacahouète, imitent la fameuse
danse de la comédie musicale du West End.

The 'Lambeth Walk', New York style, August 1938. Second on the right is Prince Sergei Obolensky, who became famous when he scored a classic Rugby try for England against the All Blacks in 1936. Obolensky died in a flying accident in 1940.

„Lambeth Walk" nach New Yorker Art, August 1938. Zweiter von rechts ist Prinz Sergei Obolensky, dessen brillantes Rugby-Spiel für die Engländer gegen die All Blacks aus Neuseeland 1936 für Furore gesorgt hatte. Obolenski kam 1940 bei einem Flugzeugabsturz ums Leben.

La version new-yorkaise de la «Lambeth Walk», août 1938. Le Prince Sergei Obolensky, deuxième à droite, devint célèbre après avoir marqué un bel essai pour l'équipe de rugby anglaise contre les All Blacks en 1936. Obolensky mourut dans un accident d'avion en 1940.

James Thomas and friends at a meeting of their smoking club, 1935. Thomas was then colonial secretary in the National Government of Great Britain. A year later his political career was in ruins when he was found guilty of divulging budget secrets.

James Thomas mit Freunden bei einem Treffen ihres Raucherclubs, 1935. Thomas war zu jener Zeit Kolonialsekretär der britischen Regierung. Ein Jahr später nahm seine politische Karriere jedoch ein jähes Ende, weil er geheime Informationen über den Staatshaushalt weitergegeben hatte.

James Thomas et des amis lors d'une réunion au fumoir de leur club, 1935. Thomas était alors secrétaire des Colonies auprès du Gouvernement national de Grande-Bretagne. L'année suivante, il fut déclaré coupable d'avoir divulgué des secrets sur le budget et sa carrière politique fut ruinée.

Society debutantes
in line as they make
their entrance at
Queen Charlotte's
Ball, London 1930.
This marked the
start of the London
Season.

Debütantinnen der
feinen Londoner
Gesellschaft beim
feierlichen Einzug
zum Ball Königin
Charlottes, 1930.
Mit ihrem Auftritt
galt die Londoner
Saison als eröffnet.

Débutantes de la
haute société en
rangs pour faire leur
entrée au bal de la
reine Charlotte,
Londres, 1930. Cet
événement marquait
l'ouverture de la
saison à Londres.

October 1938. The Pytchley Hunt hunter trials, Holdenby Mill near Spratton,
Northamptonshire. The gentlemen taking their ease are (from left to right) Lord Frederick
Pratt, J Bowlby, A Jepherson, J M Hanbury, J Kingscott and Lord Amherst of Hackney.

Oktober 1938. Das Querfeldeinrennen der Pytchley-Jagd in Holdenby Mill, nahebei
Spratton, Northamptonshire. Bei den Gentlemen, die sich eine Erfrischung gönnen,
handelt es sich (von links nach rechts) um Lord Frederick Pratt, J. Bowlby, A. Jepherson,
J. M. Hanbury, J. Kingscott und Lord Amherst of Hackney.

Octobre 1938. Chasseurs participant au concours de chasse de Pytchley, Holdenby Mill
près de Spratton, Northamptonshire. Ces gentlemen au repos sont (de gauche à droite)
Lord Frederick Pratt, J. Bowlby, A. Jepherson, J. M. Hanbury, J. Kingscott et Lord
Amherst of Hackney.

A backwater near the Henley Regatta, July 1931, photographed by Douglas Miller. As Kenneth Grahame wrote in his children's classic, *The Wind in the Willows*, 'There is nothing half so much worth doing as simply messing about in boats.'

Ein Seitenarm der Themse unweit der Stelle, an der die Regatta von Henley stattfindet, Juli 1931, fotografiert von Douglas Miller. Wie schon Kenneth Grahame in seinem Kinderbuch *The Wind in the Willows* schrieb, ist „nichts auch nur halb so schön, wie einfach in Booten herumzuschippern".

Bras mort de la rivière, non loin de l'endroit où se déroulent les Régates de Henley, juillet 1931, photographié par Douglas Miller. Kenneth Grahame écrivait dans *The Wind in the Willows*, un classique pour enfants, « Il n'y a rien qui vaille autant que de se prélasser dans un bateau ».

November 1938. A somewhat seedy London night club,
photographed by Humphrey Spender. The scene has none of
the glamour of Ciro's, Les Ambassadeurs, or the Café de
Paris. This was quite possibly a place for cads and bounders.

November 1938. Humphrey Spender fotografierte diesen
recht zwielichtigen Londoner Nachtclub. Hier fehlte der
Glamour von Ciro's, Les Ambassadeurs oder dem Café de
Paris. Er war wohl eher ein Treffpunkt der Londoner
Unterwelt.

Novembre 1938. Une boîte de nuit plutôt louche à Londres,
photographiée par Humphrey Spender. Le décor n'est pas
aussi chic que celui de Ciro's, des Ambassadeurs ou du
Café de Paris. C'était sûrement un lieu de rendez-vous pour
canailles et truands.

The cocktail lounge. The epitome of sophistication in the Thirties
– where one could get exotic mixtures such as a Gimlet, a Screwdriver,
a White Lady, a Tom Collins, or even the humble Gin and It(alian).

Eine Cocktail-Bar. Sie war in den dreißiger Jahren der Inbegriff der
Kultiviertheit. Dort konnte man solch exotische Mixgetränke genießen
wie den Gimlet, den Screwdriver, die White Lady, den Tom Collins
oder auch den bescheidenen Gin and It(alian).

Bar de luxe. La quintessence de l'élégance dans les années trente où
l'on servait des cocktails aussi exotiques que le Gimlet, le Screwdriver,
le White Lady, le Tom Collins ou, plus simplement, le Gin and
(It)alian.

New York, 1930.
A Harlem club.
'Have you seen the
well-to-do up on
Lennox Avenue, on
that famous
thoroughfare with
their noses in the
air…?'

New York, 1930.
Ein Nachtclub in
Harlem. „Habt ihr
die vornehmen
Leute gesehen, die
über die Lennox
Avenue gehen, über
diese berühmte
Straße, mit
hocherhobener
Nase …?"

New-York, 1930.
Club à Harlem.
« Avez-vous vu les
bourgeois qui
descendent l'avenue
Lennox, cette rue
célèbre, le nez en
l'air… ? »

A crowded scene at La Boule Blanche, Paris, 1930.
As George Orwell wrote in *Down and Out in Paris and
London*, 'There were tales of dope fiends, of old débauchées
in search of pretty boys, of thefts and blackmail.'

Lebhaftes Gedränge herrschte 1930 im La Boule Blanche,
Paris. George Orwell schrieb in *Erledigt in Paris und
London*, „Man erzählte sich Geschichten über
Drogensüchtige, über lüsterne alte Männer auf der Suche
nach hübschen Jungen, über Diebstahl und Erpressung."

Foule à La Boule Blanche, Paris, 1930. Dans *La Vache
enragée*, George Orwell écrivait qu'on y trouvait « des
drogués, des vieilles débauchées en mal de jolis garçons,
des voleurs et des maîtres-chanteurs. »

London, 1930. A spotlessly clean sweep. In those days chimney sweeps were regarded as bringers of good luck, and were much in demand at weddings. This particular sweep, however, may simply have been spruced up for the camera.

London, 1930. Ein blitzsauberer Schornsteinfeger. Kaminkehrer galten als Glücksbringer und waren auf Hochzeitsfeiern gerngesehene Gäste. Der hier abgebildete Herr allerdings hatte sich wohl speziell für diese Aufnahme feingemacht.

Londres, 1930. Pas une tache, tout est impeccable. A cette époque, on pensait que les ramoneurs portaient chance, et ils étaient très demandés pour les mariages. Quant à ce ramoneur, il est possible qu'il soit tiré à quatre épingles pour la photo.

A solitary pupil
amid the gleaming
glory of the new
washroom at the
Chislehurst and
Sidcup County
Secondary School,
May 1939.

Ein einsamer Schüler
im blinkenden neuen
Waschraum der
staatlichen höheren
Schule von
Chislehurst und
Sidcup, Mai 1939.

Un seul élève perdu
dans la blancheur
étincelante des
nouvelles toilettes
de l'école secondaire
du comté de
Chislehurst et
Sidcup, mai 1939.

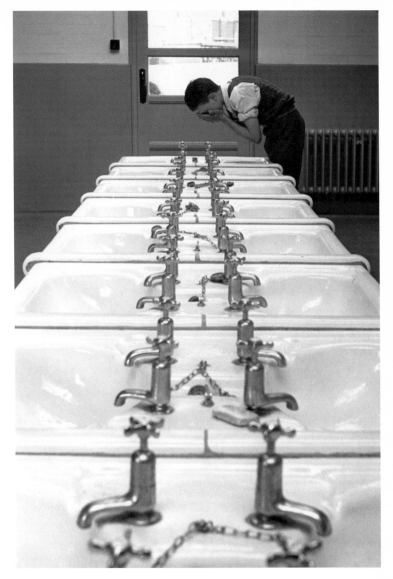

November 1939. Kurt Hutton's picture of a Wigan
dinner table. 'The basis of their diet is white bread
and margarine, corned beef, sugared tea and potatoes,'
wrote George Orwell in *The Road to Wigan Pier*.

November 1939. Eine Mahlzeit in Wigan, fotografiert
von Kurt Hutton. „Ihre Ernährung besteht im wesent-
lichen aus Weißbrot mit Margarine, Corned Beef, Tee
mit Zucker und Kartoffeln", schrieb George Orwell in
Der Weg nach Wigan Pier.

Novembre 1939. Un repas à Wigan, Angleterre,
photographié par Kurt Hutton. « Le pain blanc, la
margarine, le corned-beef, le thé sucré et les pommes de
terre étaient leur alimentation de base » écrivait George
Orwell dans *La Route qui mène au quai Wigan*.

The inside of a
typical Thirties store
cupboard or larder,
1935. As Orwell
pointed out, 'When
you are unemployed,
you want something
a little bit tasty.'

Ein Blick in einen
typischen Vorrats-
schrank der
dreißiger Jahre,
1935. „Wenn man
arbeitslos ist, möchte
man wenigstens
etwas Schmackhaftes
essen", bemerkte
Orwell.

1935. L'intérieur
d'un garde-manger
typique des années
trente. Comme
l'avait fait remarquer
Orwell, « quand on
est au chômage, on
n'a pas envie de
manger des choses
fades. »

3. Unrest
Unruhen
Agitations

Grandmother, mother and daughter – three
generations of the same family – arrive in Valencia,
refugees from the Spanish Civil War, 1937.

Drei Generationen – Großmutter, Mutter und
Tochter – bei ihrer Ankunft in Valencia auf der
Flucht vor dem Spanischen Bürgerkrieg, 1937.

Grand-mère, mère et fille – trois générations d'une
même famille – arrivent à Valence. Elles sont des
réfugiées de la Guerre d'Espagne, 1937.

3. Unrest
Unruhen
Agitations

Many saw it coming. A few tried to prevent it. In the end, it seemed there was nothing anyone could do to stop Europe plunging headlong into war.

The decade had seen troubles everywhere – in India, where the British Raj came increasingly under nationalist pressure; in Africa; in the Far East, where Japan embarked on a period of imperial expansion; even in the Americas, where there were revolts in Brazil and Cuba. In many places the spectre of a Bolshevik-type revolution raised its ugly or inspiring head (depending on your politics), but the Old Guard was usually strong enough to beat it down. Generally, left and right showed little understanding of each other and even less mercy.

Spain was the first to suffer the horrors of a modern, full-scale civil war. General Francisco Franco led a coalition of discontented military and religious traditionalists who refused to accept the legally elected Republican government of 1932. Six years later his cold-hearted rule was absolute.

In 1935 Italy invaded and conquered Ethiopia – the last time a European power grabbed a new colony by force. Elsewhere there were riots and pitched battles on the streets, in the squares and piazzas, and outside the factory gates of every major city in the world.

Viele sahen ihn kommen, doch nur wenige versuchten, ihn zu verhindern, und schließlich schien für Europa kein Weg mehr am Krieg vorbeizuführen.

In den dreißiger Jahren hatte es überall auf der Welt Unruhen gegeben: In Indien, wo die britische Oberherrschaft von seiten der Nationalisten zunehmend unter Druck gesetzt wurde. In Afrika. Im Fernen Osten, wo Japan seine Expansionspolitik verstärkte. Sogar in Mittel- und Südamerika, wo es auf Kuba und in Brasilien zu Aufständen kam. Vielerorts hob das Gespenst der bolschewistischen Revolution sein Haupt empor, doch die Alte Garde war meist stark genug, es niederzuringen. Im großen und ganzen zeigten Linke wie Rechte wenig Verständnis füreinander und noch weniger Gnade.

Spanien sollte als erstes Land die Schrecken eines modernen Bürgerkrieges kennenlernen. General Francisco Franco vereinte unter seiner Führung ein unzufriedenes Militär und religiöse Traditionalisten, die es ablehnten, die rechtmäßig gewählte republikanische Regierung von 1932 anzuerkennen. Bereits sechs Jahre später sollte Franco zum absolutistischen Herrscher aufsteigen.

Im Jahre 1935 marschierten die Italiener in Äthiopien ein. Es war das letzte Mal, daß ein europäischer Staat mit Gewalt eine neue Kolonie an sich riß. Doch auch andernorts gab es Unruhen und offene Kämpfe – in den Straßen, auf den Plätzen und vor den Fabriktoren jeder größeren Stadt der Welt.

Beaucoup l'avaient prédite mais peu tentèrent de l'éviter. A la fin, rien ni personne ne pouvait plus, semblait-il, empêcher l'Europe de basculer dans la guerre.

Cette décennie connut des conflits un peu partout : en Inde, où l'Empire britannique subissait la pression croissante des nationalistes, en Afrique, en Extrême-Orient où le Japon entrait dans une période d'expansionnisme impérial, et même en Amérique du Sud où des révoltes éclataient au Brésil et à Cuba. En bien des lieux, le spectre d'une révolution de type bolchévique était agité, menaçant ou porteur d'espoir (selon les convictions politiques), mais la vieille garde était en principe assez forte pour résister. D'une manière générale, la gauche comme la droite faisaient preuve de peu de compréhension réciproque et encore moins d'indulgence.

L'Espagne fut la première à souffrir des horreurs d'une guerre civile moderne et totale. Le général Franco était à la tête d'une coalition de militaires et de religieux traditionalistes qui refusaient de reconnaître le gouvernement républicain élu en toute légalité en 1932. Six ans plus tard, son pouvoir était impitoyable et absolu.

En 1935, l'Italie envahit et conquit l'Ethiopie – ce fut la dernière fois qu'une puissance européenne s'emparait d'une nouvelle colonie par la force. Ailleurs, des émeutes et des bagarres éclataient dans les rues, sur les places et aux portes des usines de toutes les grandes villes du monde.

10 September 1939. One week after the outbreak of
World War II, Nazi troops march in Nuremberg. The
parade was held to celebrate the Nazi Congress in that city.

10. September 1939. Anläßlich des Parteitages in
Nürnberg marschieren eine Woche nach Ausbruch des
Zweiten Weltkrieges nationalsozialistische Truppen in einer
Festparade.

10 septembre 1939. Une semaine après le début de la
Seconde Guerre mondiale, des soldats nazis défilent dans
Nuremberg pour célébrer la tenue du congrès national-
socialiste dans cette ville.

Chancellor Adolf Hitler, flanked by storm-troopers, marches into Bückeburg, near Hanover, in 1934. Like all Nazi parades, the event was stage-managed with great panache.

Reichskanzler Adolf Hitler hält 1934 Einzug in Bückeburg bei Hannover, flankiert von Männern der SA. Wie alle Nazi-Paraden wurde auch dieses Ereignis mit großem Aufwand in Szene gesetzt.

Le chancelier Adolf Hitler, encadré par des troupes d'assaut, entre dans Bückeburg, près de Hanovre, en 1934. Chaque défilé nazi était un événement mis en scène à grand renfort de panache.

1930. A fascist organization of young girls, *Giovani Italiane*, on parade. By this time, Mussolini had been in complete control of Italy for eight years and, according to Pope Pius X, had 'God's full protection'.

1930. Eine faschistische Organisation junger Mädchen, die „Giovani Italiane", bei einer Parade. Seit acht Jahren bereits beherrschte Mussolini Italien und genoß, laut Papst Pius X., „den umfassenden Schutz Gottes".

1930. Défilé des « Giovani Italiane », une organisation fasciste de jeunes filles. Mussolini disposait depuis huit ans de tous les pouvoirs en Italie et était, selon le Pape Pie X, « sous l'entière protection de Dieu ».

March 1935. Adolf Hitler inspects a guard of honour. The occasion was the official reception of the new Polish ambassador, a man destined to have unhappy relations with Germany's chancellor.

März 1935. Adolf Hitler bei der Inspektion einer Ehrenwache kurz vor dem offiziellen Empfang des neuen polnischen Botschafters, dessen Beziehungen zum Reichskanzler Deutschlands einer unglücklichen Zukunft entgegensahen.

Mars 1935. Adolf Hitler passe en revue une garde d'honneur à l'occasion de la réception officielle donnée pour le nouvel ambassadeur de Pologne, un homme dont les relations avec le chancelier allemand allaient être malheureuses.

Nazi swastikas are hung out to dry after being well-laundered, 1935. It was the year when increasingly harsh laws were enacted against the Jews, Hitler formally renounced the Treaty of Versailles, and opposition to the Nazis became grounds for divorce.

Sorgfältig gewaschene Hakenkreuzfahnen werden 1935 zum Trocknen aufgehängt. In jenem Jahr erließ die Regierung noch strengere Gesetze gegen die Juden. Hitler schwor formell dem Versailler Vertrag ab und der Widerstand gegen das Naziregime führte unweigerlich zur Entzweiung.

Des croix gammées nazies mises à sécher après la lessive, 1935. Cette année-là, des lois encore plus sévères furent mises en place à l'encontre des Juifs. Hitler dénonça formellement le Traité de Versailles. L'opposition au régime nazi devint un motif de divorce.

September 1935.
Sculptors work on
the official symbol
of the Nazi Party
Congress, to be
hung outside the
Nuremberg Opera
House.

September 1935.
Bildhauer arbeiten
am offiziellen
Symbol des
Reichsparteitages,
das später die
Fassade des
Nürnberger
Opernhauses
schmücken sollte.

Septembre 1935.
Des sculpteurs
travaillent sur
l'emblème officiel du
congrès du parti nazi
qui doit décorer la
façade de l'Opéra de
Nuremberg.

10 November 1936. Red-draped pylons topped with flaming bowls, each depicting the name of a dead Nazi hero, provide the setting for Hitler and Goering. The occasion was the 13th anniversary of the Munich Beer Hall Putsch.

10. November 1936. Am 13. Jahrestag des Hitlerputsches von München ziehen Hitler und Göring in die Stadt ein. Auf mit rotem Tuch verkleideten Pfeilern ruhen lodernde Schalen, die die Namen gefallener Nazi-Helden tragen.

10 novembre 1936. Drapés de rouge et surmontés d'une flamme, ces piliers, qui portent chacun le nom d'un héros nazi mort, servent de décor pour la venue de Hitler et Goering. Cet événement marquait le 13e anniversaire du putsch de Munich.

Mounted *Carabinieri* (military police) parade through a
triumphal arch in Rome, 1938. The march was to honour
the foundation of the German-Italian military axis.

Berittene *Carabinieri* (Militärpolizei) ziehen 1938 bei
einer Parade durch den Triumphbogen in Rom, um die
militärische Achse Deutschland-Italien zu feiern.

Défilé de la police militaire, *Carabinieri*, sous un arc de
triomphe à Rome, 1938. Il devait rendre honneur à la
création de l'axe militaire entre l'Allemagne et l'Italie.

Destined to become the two most hated men in the world, Hitler and Mussolini enjoy a tour of Florence in an open car, May 1938. They shared a mutual love of pomp and ceremony, though Hitler had none of Mussolini's style as a dancer.

Hitler und Mussolini, die die meistgehaßten Männer der Welt werden sollten, genießen eine Rundfahrt durch Florenz, Mai 1938. Beide Staatsoberhäupter liebten pompöse Auftritte und Zeremonien, Hitler besaß jedoch nicht im entferntesten Mussolinis Format als Tänzer.

Promis à devenir les deux hommes les plus haïs de la terre, Hitler et Mussolini apprécient un tour de Florence à bord d'une voiture découverte, mai 1938. Ils avaient tous deux un goût prononcé pour le faste et les cérémonies, mais Hitler était piètre danseur auprès de Mussolini.

Marshal Joseph Stalin adjusts the wipers on the windscreen
of his car, 1930. By this time he was recognized as Lenin's
successor and sole leader of the Soviet Union.

Marschall Joseph Stalin richtet die Scheibenwischer seines
Wagens, 1930. Zu dieser Zeit erkannte man ihn bereits als
Lenins Nachfolger und alleiniges Oberhaupt der
Sowjetunion an.

Le maréchal Joseph Staline ajuste les essuie-glaces du pare-
brise de sa voiture, 1930. A cette époque, il était reconnu
comme le successeur de Lénine et le seul dirigeant de
l'Union soviétique.

Another setting, another costume. Mussolini poses dressed in the uniform of the National Italian Militia, 1939.

Eine andere Szene, ein anderes Kostüm. Mussolini posiert 1939 in der Uniform der italienischen Landesmiliz.

Autre décor, autre costume. Mussolini prend la pose, vêtu de l'uniforme de la Milice nationale italienne, 1939.

Hermann Goering with a dead elk in East Prussia, 1930. Goering had been a fighter pilot and air ace in World War I, and became one of the first to join Hitler in the formation of the Nazi party.

Hermann Göring mit einem erlegten Elch in Ostpreußen, 1930. Im Ersten Weltkrieg war Göring ein Jagdfliegeras gewesen. Er gehörte zu den ersten, die sich Hitler bei der Gründung der nationalsozialistischen Partei anschlossen.

Hermann Goering posant avec un élan mort dans l'est de la Prusse, 1930. Pilote de chasse chevronné durant la Première Guerre mondiale, Goering fut l'un des premiers à rallier Hitler lors de la création du parti nazi.

Alfred Rosenberg in full flow in a German street, 1932. Rosenberg was a Nazi propagandist and writer who had joined the party in 1920. He was hanged for war crimes at Nuremberg in 1946.

Alfred Rosenberg in Aktion auf einer deutschen Straße, 1932. Der national-sozialistische Schriftsteller und Propagandist Rosenberg war 1920 in die Partei eingetreten und wurde 1946 in Nürnberg für seine Kriegsverbrechen gehängt.

Alfred Rosenberg en plein discours dans une rue allemande, 1932. Propagandiste et écrivain nazi, Rosenberg avait adhéré au parti dès 1920. Il fut pendu pour crimes de guerre à Nuremberg en 1946.

Joseph Goebbels, like Rosenberg, was a bitter anti-Semite and a master of mob oratory. When this picture was taken, in 1935, he was head of the so-called Ministry of Public Enlightenment and Propaganda.

Joseph Goebbels war wie Rosenberg ein erbitterter Antisemit und meisterhafter Volksredner. Als diese Aufnahme 1935 entstand, oblag ihm die Leitung des sogenannten Ministeriums für Volksaufklärung und Propaganda.

Joseph Goebbels, tout comme Rosenberg, était un antisémite farouche et un orateur démagogue de grand talent. Au moment où ce cliché fut pris, en 1935, il était à la tête de ce qu'on appelait le ministère de l'Information et de la Propagande.

Germany, 1935. The sign carried by the woman reads, 'I am the greatest
swine and only get myself mixed up with Jews!' The sign carried by the
man reads, 'I am a Jew, I only take German girls to my room!'

Deutschland, 1935. Auf dem Schild, das man der Frau umgehängt hat,
steht geschrieben: „Ich bin am Ort das größte Schwein und laß mich nur
mit Juden ein!", auf dem des Mannes ist zu lesen: „Ich nehme als
Judenjunge immer nur deutsche Mädchen mit aufs Zimmer!"

Allemagne, 1935. La pancarte que tient la femme dit « Je suis la plus
grande des salopes et je ne fréquente que des Juifs! » et celle de l'homme
« Je suis juif et je n'emmène que des Allemandes dans ma chambre! »

The introduction of a boycott of Jewish goods in Germany, April 1933. Nazi pickets carry banners proclaiming, 'Germans! Defend yourselves! Don't buy from Jews!' Goebbels attempted to convince the rest of the world that the campaign was a spontaneous outburst of public opinion.

Im April 1933 rufen die Nazis zum Boykott jüdischer Waren auf. Sie tragen Schilder mit der Aufschrift: „Deutsche! Wehrt Euch! Kauft nicht mehr bei Juden!" Goebbels versuchte, die Weltöffentlichkeit davon zu überzeugen, daß diese Kampagne der Meinung der Bevölkerung entsprach und von ihr ausgegangen war.

Mise en place du boycott des produits juifs en Allemagne, 1933. Des nazis font le piquet avec des pancartes qui proclament « Allemands ! Défendez-vous ! N'achetez rien chez les Juifs ! » Goebbels tenta de convaincre le reste du monde que cette campagne n'était qu'une manifestation spontanée de l'opinion publique.

Friedrichstraße, Berlin, 11 November 1938 – two days after *Kristallnacht* (the 'Night of Broken Glass'). The reason for the sudden violence against Jewish property was allegedly the murder of Ernst vom Rath, a third secretary at the German embassy in Paris.

Friedrichstraße, Berlin, am 11. November 1938 – zwei Tage nach der Kristallnacht. Als Grund für die plötzlichen Übergriffe auf jüdisches Eigentum wurde die Ermordung von Ernst vom Rath, des dritten Sekretärs der deutschen Botschaft in Paris, vorgeschoben.

Friedrichstraße, Berlin, 11 novembre 1938 – deux jours après la *Kristallnacht* (la Nuit de Cristal). Cette soudaine violence à l'encontre des biens juifs fut, dit-on, causée par le meurtre d'Ernst vom Rath, troisième secrétaire à l'Ambassade d'Allemagne à Paris.

The morning after
Kristallnacht. More
than 90 people were
killed, most of them
Jewish merchants.

Der Morgen nach
der Kristallnacht.
Über 90 Menschen
wurden getötet, von
denen die meisten
jüdische Kaufleute
waren.

Le lendemain de la
Nuit de Cristal. Plus
de 90 personnes ont
été tuées, la plupart
étaient des
commerçants juifs.

The Irish fascist politician Owen O'Duffy at a meeting of the Blue Shirts
in Bandon, near Cork, Ireland, 1934. Although there was considerable
anti-British feeling in Ireland, the Blue Shirts had very little influence.

Der faschistische irische Politiker Owen O'Duffy bei einer Zusammen-
kunft der Blauhemden in Bandon bei Cork, 1934. Obwohl in Irland ein
beträchtliches Maß an anti-britischer Stimmung herrschte, besaßen die
Blauhemden kaum Einfluß.

Owen O'Duffy, un fasciste irlandais, lors d'une réunion des Chemises
bleues à Bandon, près de Cork, en Irlande, 1934. Bien que l'Irlande fût
profondément anti-britannique, l'influence des Chemises bleues
demeura très faible.

Sir Oswald Mosley inspects his Black Shirts in London. Mosley was the founder of the British Union of Fascists, an extreme right-wing group with a membership of 20,000. In 1936, when this photograph was taken, the British government banned the wearing of political uniforms.

Sir Oswald Mosley, der Begründer des Britischen Faschistenbundes, bei der Inspektion seiner Schwarzhemden in London. Die „British Union of Fascists" hatte etwa 20.000 Mitglieder. 1936, als diese Aufnahme entstand, verbot die britische Regierung das Tragen von Parteiuniformen.

Sir Oswald Mosley passe en revue ses Chemises noires à Londres. Mosley fonda le parti fasciste britannique, un groupe d'extrême-droite comptant 20 000 membres. En 1936, date à laquelle cette photographie fut prise, le gouvernement britannique décida d'interdire le port des uniformes politiques.

The Battle of Cable Street, London, October 1936. Police dismantle road barricades made by communists to prevent Mosley's Black Shirts marching into the predominantly Jewish heart of the East End. The police were under orders to help Mosley, but the march was abandoned.

Die Schlacht der Cable Street, London, Oktober 1936. Polizisten beseitigen Straßensperren, die Kommunisten errichtet hatten, um Mosleys Schwarzhemden am Einmarsch in den überwiegend jüdischen Kern des Londoner East Ends zu hindern. Die Polizei hatte Anweisung, Mosleys Vorhaben zu unterstützen, der Marsch wurde jedoch abgebrochen.

La Bataille de Cable Street, Londres, octobre 1936. La police démonte les barricades élevées par les communistes pour empêcher l'entrée des Chemises noires de Mosley dans ce quartier de l'East End, surtout habité par des Juifs. La police avait reçu l'ordre de protéger Mosley mais les manifestants abandonnèrent en cours de route.

A protester – almost
certainly left-wing
– is led away by
police after a scuffle
in the Battle of
Cable Street.

Polizisten führen
einen Demonstran-
ten, wahrscheinlich
einen Kommunisten,
nach einem Hand-
gemenge während
der Schlacht der
Cable Street ab.

Un manifestant, très
certainement de
gauche, est emmené
par la police après
une échauffourée,
le jour de la Bataille
de Cable Street.

Spain, November 1936. Captured Republican troops are marched away by
Nationalists on the Samosierra front. George Orwell, who fought on the
Republican side, wrote, 'They were gnarled, rustic-looking men, shepherds
or labourers from the olive groves...'– *Homage to Catalonia*.

Spanien, November 1936. Nationalisten treiben gefangene republikanische
Soldaten an der Front von Samosierra zusammen. „Es waren rauhe
Männer mit groben Gebärden vom Lande, Schäfer oder Arbeiter aus den
Olivenhainen ..." schrieb George Orwell, der auf der Seite der
Republikaner kämpfte, in *Mein Katalonien*.

Espagne, novembre 1936. Des soldats républicains, faits prisonniers par les
Nationalistes, sont emmenés sur le front de la Samosierra. George Orwell,
qui combattit aux côtés des républicains, écrivit que « c'était des hommes
grossière et d'allure rudes,... des bergers ou des paysans venus des
oliveraies... » dans *Hommage à la Catalogne*.

Women snipers in the Spanish Civil War, 1936.
Few Spaniards escaped the horrors of the war,
which covered practically the whole country.

Weibliche Heckenschützen im Spanischen
Bürgerkrieg, 1936. Die Schrecken des Krieges
überzogen praktisch ganz Spanien.

Des femmes prêtes à tirer pendant la Guerre
d'Espagne, 1936. Peu d'Espagnols échappèrent
aux horreurs de la guerre qui fut livrée dans
presque tout le pays.

A French soldier helps to carry a Spanish refugee's baggage
through a pass in the Pyrenees, 1936. Little assistance came to
the Republicans from the British or French governments.

Ein französischer Soldat hilft 1936 einer flüchtenden
Spanierin, ihr Gepäck über einen Paß in den Pyrenäen zu
tragen. Weder die britische noch die französische Regierung
leistete den Republikanern nennenswerte Hilfe.

Un soldat français porte la valise d'une réfugiée espagnole
franchissant un col des Pyrénées, 1936. Les républicains ne
reçurent pratiquement aucun soutien de la part des
gouvernements français ou britannique.

Spanish refugees, 1939. In January of that year, Franco's victorious troops
entered Barcelona and the war was virtually over. More than 400,000 people
had been killed. Hundreds of thousands more fled from their homeland.

Spanische Flüchtlinge, 1939. Im Januar jenes Jahres waren Francos siegreiche
Truppen in Barcelona einmarschiert und hatten den Krieg beendet. Mehr als
400.000 Menschen waren ums Leben gekommen, weitere Hunderttausende
aus ihrem Heimatland geflohen.

Réfugiés espagnols, 1939. En janvier de cette année-là, les troupes
victorieuses de Franco entrèrent dans Barcelone. La guerre était presque
finie. Plus de 400 000 personnes furent tuées. Des centaines de milliers
d'autres fuirent leur pays.

British soldiers hurry to quell yet another riot in the old city of Jerusalem, October 1938. It took 11 infantry battalions and a cavalry regiment to maintain order in the face of Palestinian Arab unrest.

Britische Soldaten eilen in die Altstadt von Jerusalem, um erneut einen Aufstand niederzuschlagen, Oktober 1938. Mit 11 Infanterie-Bataillonen und einem Kavallerie-Regiment wurden angesichts der Unruhen der palästinensischen Araber Gesetz und Ordnung aufrechterhalten.

Soldats britanniques partent réprimer une nouvelle émeute dans la vieille ville de Jérusalem, octobre 1938. Il fallut 11 bataillons d'infanterie et un régiment de cavalerie pour maintenir l'ordre face aux agitateurs palestiniens.

Unrest in India, February 1932. Police try to control crowds in Delhi after a Congress Party procession had been broken up by demonstrators. The Congress Party had been banned the month before and its leader, Gandhi, had been jailed.

Unruhen in Indien, Februar 1932. Polizisten versuchen in Delhi, die aufgebrachte Menschenmenge zu beruhigen, nachdem ein Umzug der Kongreßpartei von Demonstranten gestört und abgebrochen worden war. Die Kongreßpartei war einen Monat zuvor verboten und ihr Vorsitzender, Mahatma Gandhi, verhaftet worden.

Emeute en Inde, février 1932. La police tente de contenir la foule à Delhi après un défilé du Parti du Congrès, interrompu par des manifestants. Le Parti du Congrès avait été interdit quelques mois plus tôt et son dirigeant, Gandhi, emprisonné.

By 1930, when this photograph was taken, Mohandas Gandhi had emerged as the leader of political opposition to British rule in India. He is leading the 200-mile-long Salt March, which symbolically defied the government monopoly on salt production.

1930, als diese Aufnahme entstand, hatte Mahatma Gandhi bereits die Führung der politischen Opposition gegen die britische Oberherrschaft in Indien übernommen und leitete den 320 Kilometer langen „Salz-Marsch", der symbolisch das Regierungs-monopol brechen sollte.

1930, ce cliché fut pris alors que Gandhi s'imposait déjà comme le chef de l'opposition au régime britannique en Inde. Cette année-là, il conduisit la Marche du sel, longue de 320 kilomètres, pour défier symboliquement le monopole du gouvernement.

In 1931, Gandhi came to Britain to attend the London round-table conference on Indian constitutional reform. He also took time out to visit King George and Queen Mary, and (here) the women of Darwen, Lancashire.

1931. Gandhi reiste nach Großbritannien, um an der Londoner Konferenz über die indische Verfassungsreform teilzunehmen. Er besuchte auch König Georg und Königin Maria sowie (hier) die Frauen von Darwen in Lancashire.

En 1931, Gandhi se rendit à Londres pour participer à la table ronde sur la réforme de la constitution indienne. Il prit aussi le temps de rendre visite au roi Georges et à la reine Marie et à des femmes (ici) de Darwen, Lancashire.

After a Japanese air raid on the South railway station,
Shanghai, 1937. The Sino-Japanese War had been spluttering
for six years, but intensified in 1937 with the Japanese
seizure of Manchuria.

Nach einem japanischen Luftangriff auf den Südbahnhof in
Shanghai, 1937. Der Krieg zwischen China und Japan zog
sich bereits sechs Jahre lang hin und intensivierte sich 1937
mit der Besetzung der Mandschurei durch die Japaner.

Après un raid japonais sur la gare Sud de Shangaï, 1937.
La guerre sino-japonaise durait depuis six ans mais s'intensifia
en 1937 après la conquête de la Mandchourie par le Japon.

Civilians flee in panic during a Japanese air raid on Canton, June 1938. It took less than two years for the better-armed, better-trained Japanese military to overrun much of China.

Zivilisten fliehen in panischer Angst während eines Luftangriffs der Japaner auf Kanton, Juni 1938. Das besser bewaffnete und besser ausgebildete japanische Militär brauchte weniger als zwei Jahre, um große Teile Chinas zu besetzen.

Des civils paniqués fuient durant un raid japonais sur Canton, juin 1938. Il fallut moins de deux ans à l'armée japonaise, mieux équipée et mieux entraînée, pour occuper une grande partie de la Chine.

A panorama of the Zabei district of Shanghai after it had been bombed by Japanese planes in 1937. Shelling and raids such as this provoked widespread panic among the Chinese, who swarmed round the foreign concessions, hoping for shelter.

Der Zabei-Distrikt von Shanghai nach einem japanischen Luftangriff im Jahre 1937. Granatbeschuß und Bombenabwürfe verbreiteten Panik unter den Chinesen. Sie suchten Schutz in der Nähe von ausländischen Firmengeländen und Botschaften, die nicht bombardiert wurden.

Vue sur le quartier de Zabei à Shanghai bombardé par l'aviation japonaise en 1937. Les tirs d'obus et les bombardements, comme celui-ci, provoquèrent une grande panique parmi les Chinois qui fuirent en masse vers les concessions étrangères, espérant pouvoir y trouver refuge.

'Happy days are here again ...' (Roosevelt campaign song). Franklin Delano
Roosevelt's landslide presidential victory in 1932 promised a New Deal for the
American people. 'I am waging a war', he declared, 'against Destruction, Delay,
Deceit and Despair.'

„Eine glückliche Zeit bricht an ...", so lautete die Hymne der Wahlkampagne von
Franklin Delano Roosevelt. Mit seinem überwältigenden Sieg bei der Präsident-
schaftswahl von 1932 versprach er der amerikanischen Bevölkerung ein neues
politisches Programm (New Deal). „Ich nehme den Kampf auf", erklärte er,
„gegen die Zerstörung, die Verzögerung, den Betrug und die Verzweiflung."

« Les beaux jours sont revenus ... » était le refrain de la campagne de Franklin
Delano Roosevelt. La victoire écrasante de Roosevelt aux présidentielles de 1932
promettait une « nouvelle donne » (New Deal) au peuple américain. « J'entre en
guerre », déclarait-il, « contre la destruction, la retard, la malhonnêté et le désespoir ».

Members of the
'Bonus Army',
World War I
veterans who
demanded payment
of a war 'bonus'
promised by
Congress, camp out
on the grounds of
the Capitol, July
1932.

Mitglieder der
„Bonus Army",
Veteranen des Ersten
Weltkriegs, die die
Auszahlung des vom
Kongreß ver-
sprochenen „Bonus"
forderten, kam-
pieren auf dem
Gelände des
Kapitols, Juli 1932.

Des membres de la
« Bonus Army »,
vétérans de la
Première Guerre
mondiale, qui
réclamaient le
paiement de la
« bonus » promise
par le Congrès,
campent aux abords
du Capitole, Juillet
1932.

The Duke and Duchess of Windsor
(formerly Edward VIII and Mrs Simpson)
pose at their temporary home in Sussex,
1939. Their wish to marry led to the
abdication crisis three years earlier.
Churchmen, politicians and newspaper
owners objected to the king marrying a
divorced American commoner.

Der Herzog und die Herzogin von
Windsor (der ehemalige König Edward
VIII. und Mrs. Simpson) posieren in ihrem
zeitweiligen Heim in Sussex, 1939. Ihr
Wunsch zu heiraten, hatte drei Jahre zuvor
die Abdankungskrise eingeleitet, denn die
Kirchenoberhäupter, Politiker und auch
Zeitungsverleger tolerierten nicht, daß der
König eine geschiedene bürgerliche
Amerikanerin ehelichte.

Le duc et la duchesse de Windsor
(ex-Edouard VIII et Mme Simpson) posent
pour les photographes devant leur
résidence temporaire du Sussex, 1939.
Leur désir de se marier avait entraîné
l'abdication du roi trois ans plus tôt.
L'Eglise, les politiciens et les magnats de la
presse s'étaient opposés au mariage du roi
avec une roturière américaine et divorcée.

A demonstrator in Downing Street, London, during the abdication crisis, December 1936. Although the British press had agreed not to report what was happening, there had been enormous public speculation as to the future of Edward VIII, Mrs Simpson and the monarchy.

Ein Demonstrant in der Londoner Downing Street während der Abdankungskrise, Dezember 1936. Obwohl die britische Presse sich bereiterklärt hatte, nicht über diese Angelegenheit zu berichten, gab es in der Öffentlichkeit zahllose Spekulationen über die Zukunft Edwards VIII., Mrs. Simpsons und der Monarchie.

Manifestant à Downing Street, Londres, durant la crise gouvernementale, décembre 1936. La presse britannique avait accepté de ne dirulguer aucune information à ce sujet, mais l'opinion publique se livrait à toutes sortes de conjectures sur l'avenir d'Edouard VIII, de Mme Simpson et de la monarchie.

Patrick McMahon is
arrested after trying
to shoot Edward
VIII at Constitution
Hill, London, in July
1936.

Patrick McMahon
wird nach dem miß-
glückten Attentat auf
Edward VIII. am
Constitution Hill in
London verhaftet,
Juli 1936.

Patrick McMahon
est arrêté après
avoir tenté d'abattre
Edouard VIII à
Constitution Hill,
Londres, en juillet
1936.

4. Leisure
Freizeit
Les loisirs

June 1939. Girls at summer school, Dymchurch, south of England.
It was the last summer for six years when children would be free to
visit any of the Channel seaside resorts or beaches.

Juni 1939. Eine Gruppe von Mädchen auf einer Sommerfreizeit im
südenglischen Dymchurch. Dies war der letzte Sommer, in dem
Kinder alle Seebäder besuchen und sich an allen Stränden frei
bewegen konnten, bevor die Kanalküste sechs Jahre lang zur Ver-
teidigungszone wurde.

Juin 1939. Filles en colonie de vacances à Dymchurch, sud de
l'Angleterre. Ce fut le dernier été pour six ans durant lequel les
enfants purent profiter librement des stations balnéaires ou plages
du bord de la Manche.

4. Leisure
Freizeit
Les loisirs

In 1930 Harry Kessler wrote of a new feeling that had grown up since the end of World War I: 'To enjoy the light, the sun, happiness, their own bodies... a popular movement has taken hold of all the young people of Germany.'

This new feeling was widespread. Millions were looking for fun – by which they meant good, clean, healthy fun – something more wholesome than what the jazz-mad Twenties had lusted after. They believed that they had found it in Leagues of Health and Beauty, in New Age Dance Movements, in listening to their souls, in allowing the rhythms of the earth to enter their bodies through the soles of their feet.

Much of it was spurious, some of it was on the insane side of bizarre, but, for the first time since the days of the Romans and Ancient Greeks, the ordinary people of the Western world had rediscovered the notion of *mens sana in corpore sano* ('a healthy mind in a healthy body'). Maidens leapt to the music of pipes and flutes. Naturism thrived.

If such athleticism was too much for some, there was fun and fulfilment to be found in the less exacting day trip. A quick paddle and some sea air did as much good for the spirit as any amount of Swedish drill.

Im Jahre 1930 beschrieb Harry Kessler ein neues Körpergefühl, das sich seit dem Ende des Ersten Weltkrieges entwickelt hatte: Die jungen Deutschen hatte eine Volksbewegung erfaßt, deren Ziel es war, das Licht, die Sonne, das Glück und den Körper zu genießen.

Diese neue Einstellung verbreitete sich wie ein Lauffeuer. Millionen von Menschen suchten nach Lebensfreude – womit anständiges und gesundes Amüsement gemeint war und nicht etwa das der verruchten, jazzsüchtigen zwanziger Jahre. Sie fanden es in Frauenverbänden für Gesundheit und Schönheit wie auch in Tanzbewegungen des New Age. Sie hörten auf ihre innere Stimme und erlaubten den Erdrhythmen, über die Fußsohlen in den Körper einzudringen.

Einen Großteil dieser Aktivitäten konnte man als Hokuspokus bezeichnen, manches schon beinahe als Verrücktheit, aber zum ersten Mal seit der Antike hatten die einfachen Menschen der westlichen Welt das Prinzip des *mens sana in corpore sano* (in einem gesunden Körper steckt ein gesunder Geist) wiederentdeckt. Junge Mädchen tanzten graziös zu Flötenmusik, und die Freikörperkultur blühte.

Wem solches Athletentum nicht behagte, der konnte auch Freude und Erfüllung auf einem weniger anspruchsvollen Tagesausflug finden. Ein wenig im Meer zu planschen und die Seeluft tief einzuatmen, erfrischte den Geist letztlich ebensosehr wie aufwendige schwedische Drillübungen.

En 1930, Harry Kessler évoquait un sentiment nouveau apparu dès la fin de la Première Guerre mondiale : «Profiter de la lumière, du soleil, de la joie de vivre, de son corps – un mouvement populaire qui s'est emparé de toute la jeunesse allemande.»

Ce nouvel état d'esprit était général. Des millions de gens aspiraient au plaisir, mais à un plaisir sain, propre et sportif, à quelque chose de plus complet que l'enivrement des années vingt, folles de jazz. Ils pensaient l'avoir trouvé avec les ligues de beauté et de santé et les mouvements de danse pour un âge nouveau, en écoutant leurs âmes et en laissant les rythmes de la terre pénétrer leurs corps par la plante des pieds.

Dans tout cela, beaucoup était feint, pour ne pas dire étrange mais, pour la première fois depuis l'Antiquité romaine et grecque, les gens ordinaires du monde occidental redécouvraient le concept *mens sana in corpore sano* (un esprit sain dans un corps sain). Les jeunes filles dansaient au son des pipeaux et des flûtes et le naturisme fleurissait un peu partout.

Ceux qui restaient indifférents à ce type d'expression corporelle s'adonnaient aux joies de l'excursion, moins contraignantes et tout aussi enrichissantes. Enfin, une petite baignade et un peu d'air frais au bord de la mer faisaient autant de bien à l'esprit que n'importe quel exercice en vogue à l'époque.

September 1934.
A seaside novelty
– inflated airbeds on
the beach at
Margate, England.

September 1934.
Eine Neuheit erobert
den Strand. Luft-
matratzen schaukeln
in den Wellen des
englischen Seebads
Margate.

Septembre 1934.
Nouveautés sur le
bord de mer – des
matelas gonflables
sur la plage de
Margate, Angleterre.

Kurt Hutton's classic photograph of two young women on the merry-go-round at Southend Fair, England, 1939.

Diese berühmte Aufnahme von Kurt Hutton zeigt junge Frauen auf dem Jahrmarkt von Southend in England, 1939.

Un cliché célèbre de Kurt Hutton montrant deux jeunes femmes sur un manège à la foire de Southend, Angleterre, 1939.

July 1939. Deckchair slumber, Blackpool. This was the biggest and brashest of Britain's seaside resorts, though often far from warm. As comedian George Formby observed: 'They call it breezy Blackpool as everybody knows. We don't know where the wind comes from but we all know where it goes.'

Juli 1939. Siesta im Liegestuhl. Blackpool war zu jener Zeit das größte britische Seebad, und im Sommer herrschte dort Hochbetrieb – trotz der oft widrigen Witterung. Der Komiker George Formby reimte: „Man nennt es das windige Blackpool, wohin man sich auch dreht. Wir wissen nicht, wo der Wind herkommt, aber wohl, wohin er weht."

Juillet 1939. Sieste en chaise longue à Blackpool, la plus grande et la plus folle des stations balnéaires britanniques, même s'il y faisait rarement chaud. L'humoriste George Formby dit à son propos : « On l'appelle Blackpool la venteuse, c'est bien connu. On ne sait pas d'où vient le vent, mais on sait où il souffle. »

Easter 1939. Holiday couples at Runnymede camp, near London, dance to the music of a wind-up gramophone. Dancing reached the peak of its popularity in the Thirties, with couples dancing in fields, trains, on the roofs of cars, the streets, and at home.

Ostern 1939. Urlauber tanzen im Runnymede Camp bei London zur Musik eines Grammophons. Das Tanzen erreichte in den dreißiger Jahren den Höhepunkt seiner Beliebtheit – Paare tanzten auf den Feldern, in der Eisenbahn, auf Autodächern, in den Straßen und zu Hause.

Printemps 1939 au camp de vacances de Runnymede, près de Londres. Couples dansant sur la musique d'un gramophone. La danse ne fut jamais aussi populaire que dans les années trente. Les gens dansaient dans les champs, dans les trains, sur les toits des voitures, dans la rue ou chez eux.

The joys of Butlin's holiday camp, Skegness, August 1939. Skegness, on the
North Sea coast of England, was something of a joke as a resort – thanks largely
to a railway poster which (correctly) proclaimed, 'Skegness is so bracing!'

Urlaubsfreuden in Butlins Feriendorf in Skegness, August 1939. Das an der
Nordseeküste Englands gelegene Skegness wurde als Seebad eher belächelt –
nicht zuletzt wegen des Eisenbahnplakats, das (zu Recht) behauptete: „Skegness
belebt und stärkt die Abwehrkräfte!"

Les plaisirs du camp de vacances de Butlin, Skegness, août 1939. Située sur la
côte anglaise de la mer du Nord, Skegness aspirait au titre de station balnéaire –
une affiche des chemins de fer y contribuait à sa manière en proclamant (à juste
titre) : « Skegness est tellement vivifiant ! »

Easter Bank Holiday preparations, Barry Island, South Wales, 1937. Barry Island was a real bucket-and-spade resort, sandwiched between the docks and the sea, and enormously popular with miners and their families from the valleys of South Wales.

Vorbereitungen für die Osterferien, Barry Island, 1937. Barry Island war ideal für den traditionellen Urlaub mit Schaufel, Sieb und Sandeimer. Es war bei den Burgarbeiterfamilien aus den südwalisischen Tälern ungeheuer beliebt.

Préparatifs pour les vacances de Pâques, Barry Island, Pays de Galles, 1937. Coincée entre les docks et la mer, Barry Island était idéale pour faire des pâtés de sable et très appréciée des familles de mineurs dan le sud du pays de falles.

Table tennis on the rooftop of a London hostel, August
1935. The hostel was for women who worked in
the refreshment rooms at Paddington Station, London.
Their work required an early start and a late finish,
so they lived close by.

Ein Tischtennismatch auf dem Dach eines Londoner
Wohnheims, August 1935. In diesem Heim wohnten
Frauen, die in den Erfrischungsräumen des Bahnhofs
Paddington, London, arbeiteten. Da sie einen sehr
langen Arbeitstag hatten, war es wichtig, daß sie in der
Nähe wohnten.

Table de ping-pong sur le toit d'un hôtel de Londres,
août 1935. Cet hôtel était réservé aux femmes qui
travaillaient aux buffets de la gare de Paddington à
Londres. Elles devaient commencer tôt et finissaient
tard, aussi logeaient-elles tout près.

Suburban oasis – residents of Streatham in South London
keep cool in their garden pond, August 1933. It was a
wonderful summer of hot, cloudless days.

Eine Oase am Stadtrand. Einwohner des Vororts Streatham
in Süd-London genießen die Kühle ihres Gartenteichs,
August 1933. In jenem wunderbaren Sommer war der
Himmel überwiegend strahlend blau und wolkenlos.

Oasis en banlieue. Des habitants de Streatham dans le sud
de Londres se rafraîchissent dans l'étang de leur jardin,
août 1933. Ce fut un été magnifique, chaud et sans nuages.

The delights of the
solarium at Poole,
Dorset, March 1933.
The sun and its
'health-giving rays'
were almost
worshipped in the
Thirties.

Die Freuden des
Solariums in Poole,
Dorset, März 1933.
Die Sonne und ihre
gesunde Wirkung
auf den Menschen
wurde in den
dreißiger Jahren sehr
geschätzt.

Les délices du
solarium de Poole,
Dorset, mars 1933.
Le soleil et ses
rayons porteurs de
santé étaient vénérés
dans les années
trente.

Young hikers in the Lake District of England, 1935. Walking,
rambling, and climbing attracted thousands of people. Battles
were fought to gain public access to moorland and hillside.

Junge Wanderer im englischen Lake District, 1935. Tausende
von Menschen begeisterten sich für das Wandern, Klettern
oder Bergsteigen und kämpften um den öffentlichen Zugang
zu Moor- und Heidelandschaften oder hügeligem Gelände.

Jeunes randonneurs dans la région des lacs, Angleterre,
1935. Des milliers de personnes s'enthousiasmèrent pour la
marche, la randonnée et l'escalade. On se battit pour
permettre l'accès du public aux landes et collines.

Picnicking outside a tent, 1935. In the Thirties, the joys of open-
air life were experienced for the first time by millions of ordinary
people. Camping was no longer confined to the Boy Scouts.

Ein Picknick vor dem Zelt, 1935. Millionen einfacher Menschen
lernten in den dreißiger Jahren zum ersten Mal die Freuden des
Lebens in der Natur kennen, und Camping blieb nicht länger den
Pfadfindern vorbehalten.

Pique-nique devant la tente, 1935. Dans les années trente, les
joies de la vie en plein air furent pour la première fois partagées
par des millions de gens. Le camping n'était plus réservé aux
scouts.

March 1939.
Members of the
Manchester YMCA
practise for a display
of physical fitness at
the Free Trade Hall.

März 1939.
Mitglieder des
YMCA in
Manchester
trainieren für einen
Auftritt zur
Demonstration ihrer
körperlichen Fitneß
in der Free Trade
Hall.

Mars 1939. Des
membres du YMCA
de Manchester
répètent en vue
d'une démonstration
de performance
physique au Free
Trade Hall.

Southport, Lancashire, 1931. The
Albatross Swimming Club limber up at
an open-air seawater bathing pool.

Southport, Lancashire, 1931.
Mitglieder des Schwimmvereins
Albatross machen Lockerungsübungen
in einem Freibad mit Meerwasser.

Southport, Lancashire, 1931. Exercices
d'assouplissement pour les membres du
club de natation des Albatross dans une
piscine d'eau de mer découverte.

Red Square,
Moscow, 1937.
The Locomotive
Sports Club parade
in star formation at
a display by 40,000
young people.

Der Rote Platz,
Moskau, 1937.
Der Sportverein
Lokomotive Moskau
marschiert in
Sternformation bei
einer Parade, an der
40.000 junge Leute
teilnehmen.

Place Rouge,
Moscou, 1937.
Le club sportif La
Locomotive défile en
formation d'étoile
lors d'un spectacle
donné par 40 000
jeunes.

German precision gymnasts at the Berlin Olympics, 1936. Hitler
believed that the Olympic movement was a 'piece of theatre inspired
by the Jews'. Goebbels persuaded him that staging the Games in
Berlin would be in keeping with the notion of 'Strength through Joy'.

Deutsche Präzisionsgymnasten bei den Olympischen Spielen in
Berlin, 1936. Hitler war der Meinung, daß „die olympische
Bewegung ein von Juden initiiertes Theaterstück sei". Goebbels
konnte ihn jedoch davon überzeugen, daß eine Olympiade in Berlin
das nationalsozialistische Motto „Kraft durch Freude" verdeutlichen
würde.

La précision des gymnastes allemands aux Jeux olympiques de Berlin,
1936. Pour Hitler, le mouvement olympique était un spectacle
inventé par les Juifs. Goebbels parvint à le convaincre que les Jeux de
Berlin illustreraient la notion de « Force par la Joie ».

Going out clubbing, 1932. Novelist Richmal Crompton described the then popular Leagues of Health and Beauty as 'a miscellaneous assortment of weedy individuals who wore strange garments and ran through the village with skipping-ropes and Indian clubs' – *He Who Fights*.

Keulenschwünge, 1932. Der Schriftsteller Richmal Crompton beschrieb in *He Who Fights* die damals populären Frauenverbänden für Gesundheit und Schönheit als „ein zusammen-gewürfeltes Sortiment an schmächtigen Individuen, die seltsame Kleider tragen und mit Springseilen und Keulen durchs Dorf laufen".

Pas de danse, 1932. Dans *He Who Fights*, le romancier Richmal Crompton décrivait les Ligues de santé et de beauté, alors en vogue, comme « un mélange de gens à l'allure fluette, curieusement vêtus et courant à travers le village avec des cordes à sauter et des massues ».

May 1935. The Women's League of Health and Beauty
on parade in Hyde Park, London. This particular drill
was described as the 'flat back and slim waist' exercise.

Mai 1935. Der Frauenverband für Gesundheit und
Schönheit trainiert vor aller Augen im Londoner Hyde
Park. Die abgebildete Übung sollte Bauch und Taille
straffen.

Mai 1935. Une Ligue de santé et de beauté en
spectacle à Hyde Park, Londres. Cet exercice était
répertorié sous le titre « dos plat et taille fine ».

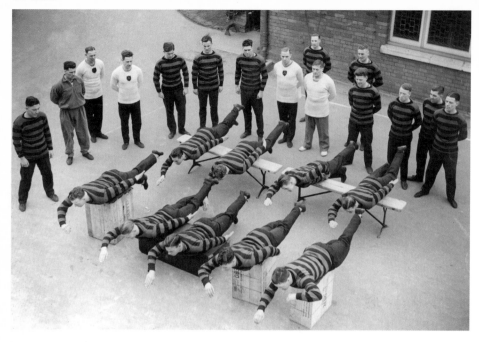

Fitness for the Forces. British soldiers
stationed at Aldershot practise their
swimming movements on dry land, March
1936. Aldershot is 30 miles from the sea.

Fitneß für die Streitkräfte. In Aldershot
stationierte britische Soldaten machen
Trockenschwimmübungen, März 1936.
Aldershot liegt etwa 50 Kilometer von der
Küste entfernt.

Mise en forme des troupes. Des soldats
britanniques de la base d'Aldershot
répètent des mouvements de natation,
mars 1936. Aldershot était située à
quelque 50 kilomètres de la mer.

Fitness for the Forces. Servicemen with the Royal
Air Force tackle the eight-foot (2.5-metre) wall
on an obstacle course at Accrington, July 1939.

Fitneß für die Streitkräfte. Angehörige der Royal
Air Force nehmen bei einer Sportveranstaltung in
Accrington eine 2,5 Meter hohe Wand in Angriff,
Juli 1939.

Mise en forme des troupes. Des militaires de
l'armée de l'air tentent d'escalader un mur haut
de 2,5 mètres lors d'une course d'obstacles sur le
terrain de sports d'Accrington, juillet 1939.

Health through Housework, 1935. The text that originally accompanied this
photograph suggested that bed-making could be done in a way that would tone the
muscles of the body. Presumably you recovered by lying on the bed afterwards.

Gesundheit durch Hausarbeit, 1935. Die ursprüngliche Bildunterschrift erklärte,
daß das Nützliche auch mit dem Gesunden verbunden werden könne. Vermutlich
erholte man sich von dem muskelstärkenden Bettenmachen, indem man sich in die
frischen Betten hineinlegte.

La forme grâce aux travaux ménagers, 1935. La légende d'origine suggérait que
faire les lits était aussi une manière de muscler son corps. Elle ne précisait pas
s'il était nécessaire ensuite de s'allonger pour récupérer.

February 1939. The Cambridge University Boat Race team join a training session of Swedish dancing. They won the race for the 14th time in 15 years.

Februar 1939. Die Rudermannschaft der Universität von Cambridge, nimmt an einer Übungsstunde in schwedischem Volkstanz teil. Sie gewann den Wettkampf zum 14. Mal innerhalb von 15 Jahren.

Février 1939. L'équipe d'aviron de l'université de Cambridge participant à une séance d'entraînement de danse suédoise. Ils gagnèrent la course pour la 14e fois en 15 ans.

Easter 1938. Fresh air and fun on the banks of the River Arun, West
Sussex. Comedian Joyce Grenfell remarked, 'Our time in the water was
strictly controlled. Some of us tended to turn blue if left in too long.'

Ostern 1938. Frischluft und Spaß am Ufer des Arun in West Sussex.
Die Komikerin Joyce Grenfell bemerkte: „Wie lange wir im Wasser
bleiben durften, wurde streng überwacht, damit niemand von uns blau
anlief."

Pâques 1938. Détente au grand air au bord de la rivière Arun, Sussex
de l'ouest. Selon l'actrice Joyce Grenfell, le temps dans l'eau était
strictement contrôlé, certains baigneurs devenant bleus de froid s'ils y
restaient trop longtemps.

'Let joy be unconfined… when Youth and
Pleasure meet' – naturists in the Swing Era, 1935.

„Laßt die Freude unbegrenzt sein, wenn Jugend
und Unbeschwertheit einander begegnen" – FKK-
Anhänger in der Ära des Swing, 1935.

« Bonheur en plein air quand Jeunesse et Plaisir
ne font qu'un » – naturistes à l'ère du swing,
1935.

The Revolution of 1937. Circus acrobats train RAF personnel in the use of
the Ayro Wheel. This was not just a piece of fun. The aim was to help airmen
learn how to avoid total disorientation when a plane went into a spin.

Die Revolution von 1937. Zirkusartisten unterrichten im Mitglieder der
Royal Air Force in der Handhabung des Rhönrads. Dabei ging es nicht nur
ums Vergnügen, sondern auch darum, den Piloten zu helfen, in einem
trudelnden Flugzeug nicht die Orientierung zu verlieren.

La Révolution de 1937. Des acrobates apprennent à des pilotes de la Royal
Air Force à se servir de la roue Ayro. C'était un moment de détente mais
aussi une manière d'aider les pilotes à ne pas être désorientés en cas de chute
en vrille.

Physical culture in the grounds of the Berlin Municipal Institute, 1935.
'The younger generation gathered in themselves an energy charged with the myth of the past, the pressure of the present, and the expectation of an unknown future' – Ernst-Werner Techow.

Körperkultur auf dem Gelände des Städtischen Instituts Berlin, 1935.
„Die junge Generation sammelte in sich eine Energie, die aus dem Mythos der Vergangenheit, dem Druck der Gegenwart und der Erwartung einer ungewissen Zukunft entstanden war", sagte Ernst-Werner Techow.

Culture physique sur le terrain de l'institut municipal de Berlin, 1935.
« La jeune génération avait une énergie tirée des mythes du passé, des tensions du présent et des espoirs d'un futur inconnu » – Ernst-Werner Techow.

Sun worship, Thirties style. A sunbather uses a reflector
to speed the process of getting a tan on the beach at
Hastings on the south coast of England, June 1938.

Sonnenanbeterin im Stil der dreißiger Jahre. Mit Hilfe
eines Reflektors versucht diese Frau ihre Bräunung am
Strand des südenglischen Hastings zu beschleunigen,
Juni 1938.

Culte du soleil, façon années trente. Une baigneuse
utilise un réflecteur pour accélérer son bronzage, à la
plage de Hastings, sud de l'Angleterre, juin 1938.

As fresh as a fruit salad – the vegetarian method of moisturizing the skin, March 1939.

Frisch wie ein Obstsalat – die vegetarische Art, der Haut Feuchtigkeit zu spenden, März 1939.

Aussi fraîche qu'une salade de fruits – la méthode végétarienne pour hydrater sa peau, mars 1939.

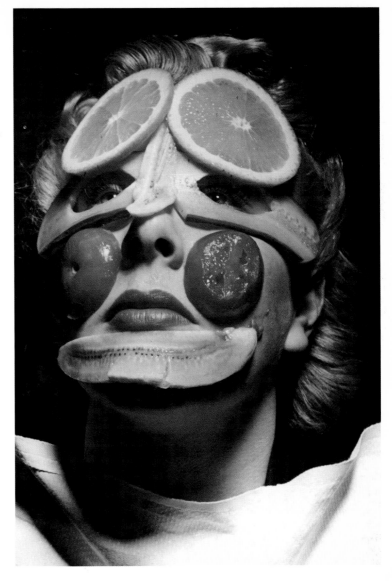

5. Cinema
Kino
Cinéma

Bette Davis at home in her Hollywood bungalow, 1935. It was the
year in which she won an Academy Award for her performance
in *Dangerous*. Davis claimed that it was she who christened such
awards 'Oscars', because she thought they resembled the backside
of her husband, whose middle name was Oscar.

Bette Davis in ihrem Bungalow in Hollywood, 1935, als ihr für
ihre schauspielerische Leistung in *Dangerous* der Academy Award
verliehen wurde. Sie behauptete, sie hätte diese Preise „Oscars"
getauft, weil sie dem Rücken ihres Ehemannes ähneln würden,
dessen zweiter Vorname Oscar war.

Bette Davis chez elle dans sa maison de Hollywood, 1935. Cette
année-là, elle obtint une Academy Award pour sa prestation dans
Dangerous. Selon Davis, c'est elle qui donna le nom d'« Oscar » à cette
récompense car elle s'était exclamée que la statuette lui rappelait son
mari de dos, et le deuxième prénom de celui-ci était Oscar.

4. Cinema
Kino
Cinéma

They didn't just move, they talked, and by mid-decade they were in glorious Technicolor.

The biggest audiences, the biggest cinemas, the biggest studios the world has ever known made up the cinema industry in the Thirties. At the centre of the celluloid dream factories was Hollywood – a rambling, scurrying dynamo run by a bunch of hard-headed businessmen who somehow managed to allow 'art' to creep into their commercial wares. There were the Warner Brothers (Jack, Harry and Albert), Harry Cohn of Columbia, Louis B Mayer, Cecil B DeMille, and Sam Goldwyn (who said of one of his films, 'I don't care if it doesn't make a nickel, I just want every man, woman and child in America to see it').

It was a glorious age, encrusted with stars: Fred Astaire and Ginger Rogers, Jean Harlow, Bette Davis, Joan Crawford, James Cagney, Humphrey Bogart, Clark Gable, Cary Grant, Greta Garbo, and the very young Judy Garland, who made *The Wizard of Oz* in 1939.

Away from Hollywood, the French cinema flourished in the hands of Jean Renoir, René Clair, Jean Vigo and others. Germany lost much of its greatest cinematic talent when Fritz Lang, Marlene Dietrich, Billy Wilder and dozens of others hurriedly left. Leni Riefenstahl, by contrast, remained, a favourite of the Nazis with her powerful propaganda films.

In den dreißiger Jahren bewegten sich die Schauspieler auf der Leinwand nicht nur, sie sprachen sogar, und um die Mitte des Jahrzehnts begeisterten sie die Kinobesucher in Technicolor.

Die Filmindustrie konnte sich zu jener Zeit der höchsten Besucherzahlen, der geräumigsten Kinosäle und der größten Filmstudios rühmen, die die Welt je gesehen hatte. Zentrum der Traumfabriken war das lebhafte Hollywood. Es wurde von einer Gruppe gewiefter Geschäftsmänner regiert, denen es auch gelang, ihrer kommerziellen Ware einen Hauch von „Kunst" zu verleihen. Zu diesen Herren gehörten die Warner Brothers (Jack, Harry und

Albert), Harry Cohn von Columbia, Louis B. Mayer, Cecil B. DeMille und Sam Goldwyn, der über einen seiner Filme sagte: „Es ist mir egal, ob der Film Geld einspielt; ich will nur, daß jeder Mann, jede Frau und jedes Kind in Amerika ihn sieht."

Den Sternenhimmel dieser glorreichen Filmzeit schmückten zahllose Stars: Fred Astaire und Ginger Rogers, Jean Harlow, Bette Davis, Joan Crawford, James Cagney, Humphrey Bogart, Clark Gable, Cary Grant, Greta Garbo und auch die junge Judy Garland, die 1939 mit *Der Magier von Oz* berühmt wurde.

In Europa erlebte das französische Kino unter Regisseuren wie Jean Renoir, René Clair und Jean Vigo eine Blütezeit. Der deutsche Film hingegen verlor seine größten Talente, als Fritz Lang, Marlene Dietrich, Billy Wilder und viele andere ihr Heimatland verließen. Leni Riefenstahl hingegen blieb in Deutschland und avancierte mit ihren einflußreichen Propagandafilmen zum Günstling der Nationalsozialisten.

Non seulement ils bougeaient et parlaient mais, au milieu des années trente, ils apparurent en couleur grâce au sensationnel procédé Technicolor.

Avec un nombre de spectateurs record, des salles de cinéma et des studios qui n'avaient jamais été aussi grands, le cinéma devint une véritable industrie dans les années trente. Au centre de cette fabrique de rêves en celluloïd il y avait Hollywood – une sorte de dynamo qui allait dans tous les sens à folle allure, dirigée par une poignée d'hommes d'affaires intraitables qui permirent néanmoins à l'« art » de se frayer un chemin. Il y avait les frères Warner (Jack, Harry et Albert), Harry Cohn de la Columbia, Louis B. Mayer, Cecil B. DeMille et Sam Goldwyn qui dit à propos de l'un de ses films : « Je m'en fiche s'il ne vaut pas un clou, tout ce que je veux c'est que chaque homme, chaque femme et chaque enfant des Etats-Unis le voient. »

L'époque fut glorieuse, illuminée par des stars comme Fred Astaire et Ginger Rogers, Jean Harlow, Bette Davis, Joan Crawford, James Cagney, Humphrey Bogart, Clark Gable, Gary Grant, Greta Garbo et la très jeune Judy Garland qui tourna *Le Magicien d'Oz* en 1939.

Loin d'Hollywood, le cinéma français florissait sous la direction de Jean Renoir, René Clair, Jean Vigo et d'autres. L'Allemagne perdit ses plus grands talents après le brusque départ de Fritz Lang, Marlene Dietrich, Billy Wilder et des dizaines d'autres. Quant à Leni Riefenstahl, elle resta et la puissance de ses films de propagande lui valut la faveur des nazis.

James Stewart and Henry Fonda at Slappy Maxie's Café, 1938.
Fonda began his career in 1935 with *A Farmer Takes a Wife*.
Stewart had just made *You Can't Take It With You* for Frank Capra.

James Stewart und Henry Fonda in Slappy Maxie's Café, 1938.
Fonda hatte seine Karriere drei Jahre zuvor mit dem Film *A Farmer Takes a Wife* begonnen und Stewart hatte gerade mit Frank Capra *You Can't Take It With You* gedreht.

James Stewart et Henry Fonda au Slappy Maxie's Café, 1938.
Fonda débuta sa carrière en 1935 dans *The Farmer takes a Wife*.
Stewart venait de terminer *You Can't Take It With You* de
Frank Capra.

Clark Gable and Carole Lombard dine with Eddie Adams (left), 1939. Lombard and Gable had just married. It was one of Hollywood's most happy marriages, until it was ended by a tragic air crash in which Lombard was killed, three years later.

Clark Gable und Carole Lombard bei einem Abendessen mit Eddie Adams (links), 1939. Lombard und Gable waren frisch vermählt. Sie führten eine der glücklichsten Ehen Hollywoods, bis die Verbindung drei Jahre später durch einen tragischen Flugzeugabsturz, bei dem Lombard ums Leben kam, ein jähes Ende fand.

Clark Gable et Carole Lombard dînent avec Eddie Adams (à gauche), 1939. Lombard et Gable venaient de se marier. Leur mariage fut l'un des plus heureux d'Hollywood mais se termina tragiquement avec la mort de Carol Lombard dans un accident d'avion trois ans plus tard.

January 1935. Sasha's portrait of Vivien Leigh at the age of 22. Three months later she appeared in a comedy called *The Mask of Virtue*, in the West End of London. It led almost immediately to a £50,000 contract with Alexander Korda.

Januar 1935. Sasha porträtierte Vivien Leigh im Alter von 22 Jahren. Drei Monate später stand sie im Londoner West End in der Komödie *The Mask of Virtue* auf der Bühne. Diese Rolle führte zu einem Vertrag über 50.000 Pfund, den sie mit Alexander Korda schloß.

Janvier 1935. Un portrait de Vivien Leigh, à 22 ans, par Sasha. Trois mois plus tard, elle jouait dans une comédie intitulée *Le Masque de la vertu* dans le West End de Londres qui lui permit peu après de signer un contrat de £ 50 000 avec Alexander Korda.

Clark Gable researches his starring role, 1939. There were those
who thought Gary Cooper might be suitable for the part of
Rhett Butler, but the general opinion in Hollywood was 'Gable
must play the role'.

Clark Gable beim Studium seiner berühmtesten Rolle, 1939.
Manche meinten zwar, daß Gary Cooper die geeignete Besetzung
für den Part des Rhett Butler sei, im allgemeinen war man
sich aber in Hollywood einig: „Gable muß die Rolle spielen."

Clark Gable étudie son rôle, 1939. Certains pensaient que
Gary Gooper ferait un bon Rhett Butler mais, de l'avis général
à Hollywood, c'était Gable qui devait avoir le rôle.

Shirley Temple,
the American child
prodigy of the
Thirties. She began
acting at the age of
three and was a star
at six.

Shirley Temple,
das amerikanische
Wunderkind der
dreißiger Jahre.
Im Alter von drei
Jahren begann sie
mit der Schau-
spielerei, mit sechs
Jahren war sie
bereits ein Star.

Shirley Temple,
le petit prodige
américain des années
trente. Elle débuta à
l'âge de trois ans et
fut une star à l'âge
de six.

Mickey Rooney and Judy Garland at the *Ice Follies* in 1936. They met at a Hollywood institution called Ma Lawlor's Professional School, where Rooney described Garland as having 'more bounce to the ounce than everyone else put together'.

Mickey Rooney und Judy Garland beim Besuch der Eislauf-Show *Ice Follies*, 1936. Sie lernten sich in der „Ma Lawlor's Professional School" (Mama Lawlors Schauspiel-schule) in Hollywood kennen. Rooney beschrieb die Garland als eine außergewöhnlich schwungvolle Person.

Mickey Rooney et Judy Garland au *Ice Follies* en 1936. Ils se rencontrèrent dans un établissement de Hollywood appelé « Ma Lawlor's Professional School », où Rooney décrivit Garland comme « quelqu'un ayant plus d'énergie que 10 personnes réunies ».

Jean Harlow, 1935. 'She moved with unfettered ease, swaggering before her men… She vamped, with humour, and when men were indifferent she did not shrug like West, or melt like Monroe, but shouted and glared' – David Shipman, *The Golden Years*.

Jean Harlow, 1935. „Sie bewegte sich mit ungehinderter Leichtigkeit, stolzierte vor den Männern hin und her… Sie spielte den Vamp, auf humorvolle Art, und wenn ein Mann nicht darauf reagierte, dann zuckte sie nicht mit den Achseln wie Mae West, schmolz auch nicht dahin wie die Monroe, sondern schrie und starrte ihn wütend an", und schrieb David Shipman in *The Golden Years*.

Jean Harlow, 1935. « Elle avançait désinvolte et crâneuse devant les hommes… Elle jouait la femme fatale avec humour et, si un homme restait indifférent, elle ne devenait pas méprisante comme West ou coquette comme Monroe, elle criait, étincelante de fureur », David Shipman, *The Golden Years*.

Greta Garbo and Nils Asther, 1932. They were both trained by Mauritz Stiller
in Sweden, and both moved to Hollywood. Garbo was a legend. Asther was
a suave romantic star whose foreign accent hindered his career in the sound era.

Greta Garbo und Nils Asther, 1932. Die waren beide Schüler bei Mauritz
Stillers in Schweden und gingen später nach Hollywood. Die Garbo wurde eine
Legende, Asther ein weltgewandter romantischer Held, dessen ausländischer
Akzent allerdings seine Karriere in der Tonfilmzeit behinderte.

Greta Garbo et Nils Asther, 1932. Tous deux formés par Mauritz Stiller en
Suède, ils partirent ensemble pour Hollywood. Garbo était une légende, Asther
une star romantique et suave dont l'accent étranger allait être un handicap
à l'avènement du film sonore.

Charles Laughton in a theatre production of *The Tempest*, 1938. Laughton
was one of the finest actors of the decade, capable of a great range of parts,
from dictators and tyrants to servants and missionaries.

Charles Laughton bei einer Theaterinszenierung von Shakespeares *Der Sturm*,
1938. Laughton war einer der größten Schauspieler dieses Jahrzehnts und
beherrschte Rollen in einer ungeheuren Bandbreite, vom Diktator und Tyrannen
bis zum Diener oder Missionar.

Charles Laughton dans une production de *La Tempête* au théâtre, 1938.
Laughton fut l'un des acteurs les plus subtils de cette décade, capable de jouer de
nombreux rôles, passant du dictateur au tyran, du domestique au missionnaire.

Randolph Scott and Cary Grant outside their Santa
Monica home, California, 1935. Cary's typically
relaxed attitude is clearly evident in the picture.

Randolph Scott und Cary Grant vor ihrem Haus in
Santa Monica, Kalifornien, 1935. Grants unbe-
kümmerte und lockere Art, für die er bekannt war,
zeigt sich deutlich auf dieser Aufnahme.

Randolph Scott et Cary Grant devant leur maison
de Santa Monica, Californie, 1935. Grant toujours
décontracté, comme le prouve ce cliché.

Loretta Young
is unmoved by the
threats of Cecil B
DeMille on the set
of *The Crusades*,
1935. DeMille was
reputedly an expert
archer.

Loretta Young wirkt
unbeeindruckt von
Cecil B. DeMilles
drohender Geste bei
den Dreharbeiten zu
The Crusades, 1935.
DeMille galt als
meisterhafter
Bogenschütze.

Loretta Young
ne craint pas le
menaçant Cecil
B. DeMille sur le
plateau *Des
Croisades*, 1935.
DeMille avait la
réputation d'être
un excellent archer.

Alfred Hitchcock, Elstree Studios, England, 1939. He was working on the shipwreck scene in *Jamaica Inn*, and used the microphone to direct the stuntmen. Graham Greene wrote of the film, 'I was irresistibly reminded of an all-star charity matinée'.

Alfred Hitchcock in den Elstree Studios, England, 1939. Er arbeitete gerade an der Schiffbruchszene von *Riff-Piraten* und gab per Mikrofon Anweisungen an die Stuntmen. Graham Greene schrieb über diesen Film: „Er erinnerte mich an eine Wohltätigkeitsmatinee mit Starbesetzung".

Alfred Hitchock aux Studios d'Elstree, Angleterre, 1939. Il utilisa un micro pour diriger les cascadeurs pendant la scène du naufrage dans *L'Auberge de la Jamaïque*. Selon Graham Greene, le film évoquait irrésistiblement « un gala de charité donné par des stars du cinéma ».

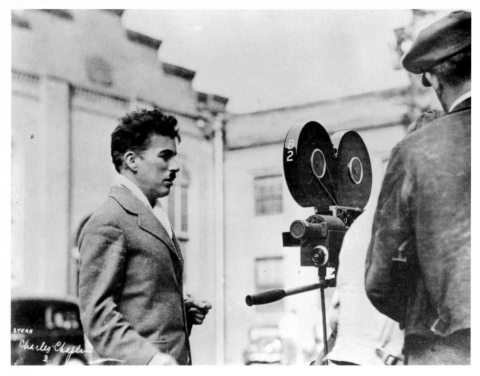

Charlie Chaplin on set, 1935. He was working on *Modern Times*, his last silent film (though he did utter a few syllables of gibberish on the sound track). It was the usual mixture of Chaplin genius and sentimentality, though *Variety* predicted it would be 'box office with a capital B'.

Charlie Chaplin bei den Dreharbeiten, 1935. Er drehte *Moderne Zeiten*, seinem letzten Stummfilm (obwohl er einige unverständliche Sätze auf Tonband aufzeichnen ließ). Der Film besaß die gewohnte Mischung aus Chaplinschem Genie und Sentimentalität, und die Zeitschrift *Variety* prophezeite ihm einen großen Kassenerfolg.

Charlie Chaplin sur le plateau, 1935. Il tournait *Les Temps modernes*, son dernier film muet (même s'il avait enregistré quelques paroles incompréhensibles sur la bande-son). Il y avait là l'habituel mélange de génie et de sentimentalisme propre à Chaplin mais, selon *Variety*, ce film « allait faire sauter le box-office ».

Gene Robert
Richea's portrait of
the Soviet director
Sergei Eisenstein,
1939.

Gene Robert Richea
porträtierte den
sowjetischen
Regisseur Sergej
Eisenstein, 1939.

Portrait du metteur
en scène soviétique
Sergei Eisenstein par
Gene Robert Richea,
1939.

1933. Stan Laurel and Oliver Hardy between scenes of Hal Roach's two-
reeler *Towed in a Hole*, directed by George Marshall and written by Laurel.
In the same year they made five other shorts and two feature-length films.

1933. Stan Laurel und Oliver Hardy bei Dreharbeiten zu Hal Roachs
Towed in a Hole. George Marshall führte Regie nach einem Drehbuch von
Stan Laurel. Im selben Jahr drehten sie noch fünf weitere Kurzfilme und
zwei Spielfilme.

1933. Stan et Oliver entre deux scènes de *Laurel et Hardy, marchands
de poisson*, dirigé par George Marshall et écrit par Laurel. La même année,
ils tournèrent cinq autres courts métrages et deux films.

Jimmy Durante
and Buster Keaton at
MGM, 1932. They
were making a
dreadful film called
*The Passionate
Plumber*.

Jimmy Durante
und Buster Keaton
in den MGM-
Studios, 1932.
Sie drehten gerade
den unsäglichen
Film *The Passionate
Plumber*.

Jimmy Durante
et Buster Keaton à
la MGM, 1932.
Ils tournaient un très
mauvais film intitulé
*Le Plombier
passionné*.

On course for
stardom. Mary Astor
on the golf links
near Hollywood,
May 1932.

Zielsicher auf dem
Weg zum Ruhm.
Mary Astor auf
einem Golfplatz in
der Umgebung von
Hollywood, Mai
1932.

Sur le chemin de
la gloire. Mary Astor
sur un parcours
de golf près
d'Hollywood, mai
1932.

Katharine Hepburn,
1935. Hepburn
really was an
accomplished
sportswoman, as she
showed in *Woman
of the Year*.

Katharine Hepburn,
1935. Die Hepburn
war eine ausgezeich-
nete Sportlerin und
stellte dies in dem
Film *Frau des Jahres*
unter Beweis.

Katharine Hepburn,
1935. Hepburn était
incontestablement
une sportive
accomplie, comme
elle le prouva dans
*La Femme de
l'année*.

James Stewart (left)
and Lew Ayres as a
pair of professional
skaters in 'Ice
Follies' of 1939. The
film was received
with appropriate
coldness.

James Stewart (links)
und Lew Ayres als
professionelle
Eiskunstläufer in
„Ice Follies", 1939.
Die Reaktion des
Publikums auf den
Film war ebenfalls
kühl.

James Stewart
(à gauche) et Lew
Ayres en patineurs
professionnels dans
« Ice Follies », 1939.
Le film fut
fraîchement
accueilli, non sans
raison.

Nils Asther (left) and
Don Alvarado,
1935. Alvarado was
an amateur boxer
and Asther a
Swedish athlete,
before both became
Hollywood stars.

Alcarado war Ama-
teurboxer und
Asther ein schwe-
discher Athlet, bevor
beide in Hollywood
Filmstars wurden.

Le Suédoise Nils
Asther (à gauche) et
Don Alvarado,
1935. Alvarado, un
ex-boxer amateur, et
Asther, un ex-
athlète, devinrent
tous les deux des
stars à Hollywood.

6. Entertainment and the arts
Unterhaltung und die schönen Künste
Les spectacles et les arts

Photographer and designer Cecil Beaton, photographed by Sasha in 1934. The picture was taken in Beaton's bathroom, where the walls were decorated with the autographed handprints of famous guests.

Sasha porträtierte den Fotografen und Designer Cecil Beaton, 1934. Die Aufnahme entstand in Beatons Badezimmer, dessen Wände mit signierten Handumrissen berühmter Gäste dekoriert waren.

Un portrait du photographe et décorateur Cecil Beaton par Sasha en 1934. Cette photographie fut prise dans la salle de bains de Beaton dont les murs étaient décorés avec les empreintes de main dessinées et signées par ses célèbres visiteurs.

6. Entertainment and the arts
Unterhaltung und die schönen Künste
Les spectacles et les arts

While the Blackshirts, Brownshirts, Blue Shirts and Red shirts marched and fought on the streets, and economies sank deeper and deeper into the financial mire, the arts flourished.

Musically there was Bartók and Stravinsky at one end of the scale, Fats Waller and Benny Goodman at the other. Somewhere in between was Duke Ellington. The greatest popular songs of all time were written by Cole Porter, George and Ira Gershwin, Rodgers and Hart, and Irving Berlin. On the classical stage, Toscanini and Furtwängler conjured magic with their batons, Kreisler and Heifetz made magic with their bows.

Galsworthy, Pirandello and Eugene O'Neill were among those who won Nobel Prizes for Literature. Aldous Huxley predicted a *Brave New World*, Ernest Hemingway believed he detected enough courage in the existing one.

Picasso still had the power to shock, but Dali and the Surrealists amazed more. The age of the square, the cube and the rectangle continued in art and architecture – from the abstractions of Mondrian, Klee and Léger to the elegant structures of Le Corbusier.

And, towards the end of the decade, when he was sorely needed, Jerry Siegel and Joe Shuster gave birth to Superman, who first appeared in *Action Comics*, 1938.

Während Schwarzhemden, Braunhemden, Blauhemden und Rothemden für ihre politischen Ideale durch die Straßen zogen und die Wirtschaftskrise immer bedrohlicher wurde, florierten die schönen Künste.

In der klassischen Musik brillierten Bartók und Strawinsky, in der leichten Muse Fats Waller und Benny Goodman – Duke Ellington lag irgendwo dazwischen. Komponisten wie Cole Porter, George und Ira Gershwin, Rodgers und Hart oder Irving Berlin schrieben die schönsten

Musical-Songs aller Zeiten. In den Konzertsälen verzauberten die Dirigenten Toscanini und Furtwängler ebenso ihr Publikum wie die Virtuosen Kreisler und Heifetz.

Zu den Gewinnern des Literaturnobelpreises gehörten Schriftsteller und Dramatiker wie Galsworthy, Pirandello oder O'Neill. Und während Aldous Huxley das Bild einer *Schönen, neuen Welt* entwarf, war Ernest Hemingway davon überzeugt, daß noch ausreichend Mut in der alten zu finden sei.

Picasso hatte bereits mit seiner Kunst die Menschen schockiert, doch Dalí und die Surrealisten versetzten ihre Betrachter in noch größeres Erstaunen. Geometrische Formen wie Quadrat, Würfel oder Rechteck inspirierten weiterhin Kunst und Architektur – von Mondrian über Klee oder Léger bis zu den Gebäuden von Le Corbusier.

Am Ende des Jahrzehnts, als die Welt ihn bitter nötig hatte, erschien Superman auf der Bild-fläche – erschaffen 1938 von Jerry Siegel und Joe Shuster für die Zeitschrift *Action Comics*.

Tandis que les Chemises noires, brunes, bleues et rouges défilaient et se battaient dans les rues, que les économies s'enfonçaient dans un marasme financier toujours plus profond, les arts florissaient.

En musique, il y avait Bartok et Stravinsky, Fats Waller et Benny Goodman, quelque part entre ces deux extrêmes, Duke Ellington. Cole Porter, George et Ira Gershwin, Rogers et Hart ainsi qu'Irving Berlin composaient des chansons vouées à un triomphe sans prévident. Dans le registre du classique, il y avait de la magie dans le bâton des chefs d'orchestre Toscanini et Furtwängler, et dans l'archer des violonistes Kreisler et Heifetz.

Le Prix Nobel de littérature fut décerné à Galsworthy, Pirandello et Eugene O'Neill, entre autres. Aldous Huxley se montrait pessimiste dans le *Meilleur des Mondes*. Quant à Ernest Hemingway, il croyait que le monde de l'époque serait à la hauteur.

Picasso savait encore choquer mais Dali et les surréalistes impressionnaient davantage. L'âge du carré, du cube et du rectangle n'était pas révolu dans l'art comme en architecture – des peintures abstraites de Mondrian, Klee et Léger aux élégantes structures de Le Corbusier.

Vers la fin de cette décennie, l'homme fort dont le monde aurait eu tant besoin apparut sous la forme de Superman, créé par Jerry Siegel et Joe Shuster et publié pour la première fois en 1938 dans *Action Comics*.

English ballerina
Leslie Burrows in
a performance of
the ballet *Fear*,
May 1932. This
photograph and
that opposite were
taken by Sasha.

Die englische
Ballerina Leslie
Burrows in einer
Aufführung des
Balletts *Fear*,
Mai 1932. Diese
Aufnahme stammt,
ebenso wie die
auf der gegenüber-
liegenden Seite, von
Sasha.

La ballerine anglaise
Leslie Burrows dans
un spectacle du
ballet *Fear*, mai
1932. Cette
photographie ainsi
que celle de la page
suivante furent
prises par Sasha.

The darling of the ballet – Margot Fonteyn in 1937. She had started as a snowflake in the Vic-Wells production of *The Nutcracker* in 1934. Three years later she was starring in a variety of roles created for her by choreographer Sir Frederick Ashton.

Der Liebling der Ballettwelt Margot Fonteyn im Jahre 1937. Sie begann ihre Karriere 1934 als Schneeflocke in *Der Nußknacker* inszeniert von Vic-Wells . Drei Jahre später begeisterte sie das Publikum in den unterschiedlichsten Hauptrollen, die ihr der Choreograph Sir Frederick Ashton auf den Leib schrieb.

La coqueluche de la danse classique – Margot Fonteyn en 1937. Elle avait débuté comme flocon de neige dans le *Casse-Noisette* produit par Vic-Wells en 1934. Trois ans plus tard, elle était la danseuse vedette de plusieurs spectacles créés pour elle par le chorégraphe Sir Frederick Ashton.

Members of the Jooss Leeder Ballet Company in a performance of the conference scene from *The Green Table* at the Old Vic, London, in August 1935. Three years earlier the ballet, a portrayal of the horrors of war, had won first prize at the Choreographic Competition in Paris.

Tänzer der Jooss Leeder Ballet Company in der Konferenzszene aus *The Green Table* in einer Aufführung am Londoner Old Vic, August 1935. Drei Jahre zuvor hatte dieses Ballett, das die Schrecken des Krieges zum Thema hatte, den ersten Preis beim Choreographischen Wettbewerb in Paris gewonnen.

Danseurs de la compagnie de ballet de Jooss Leeder dans la scène de la conférence de *La Table verte*, spectacle donné au Old Vic à Londres, août 1935. Trois ans avant, ce ballet qui relatait les horreurs de la guerre gagna le premier prix du Concours de danse de Paris.

Tilly Losch and
Roman Jasiński in a
pas de deux from
Errante at the Savoy
Theatre, London,
July 1933.

Tilly Losch und
Roman Jasiński
tanzen einen Pas de
deux aus *Errante* im
Londoner Savoy
Theatre, Juli 1933.

Tilly Losch et
Roman Jasiński
dans un pas de deux
du ballet *Errante*
donné au Savoy
Theatre, Londres,
juillet 1933.

The Jooss Leeder Ballet Company in a scene from the ballet *Inferno*, March 1935. The company, founded by German dancers Sigurd Leeder and Kurt Jooss, moved to England in 1933 and was based at Dartington Hall.

Die Jooss Leeder Ballet Company in einer Szene des Balletts *Inferno*, März 1935. Die von den deutschen Tänzern Sigurd Leeder und Kurt Jooss gegründete Balletttruppe siedelte 1933 nach England über und hatte ihren Sitz in Dartington Hall.

La compagnie de Jooss Leeder dans une scène du ballet *Inferno*, mars 1935. La compagnie fut fondée par deux danseurs allemands, Sigurd Leeder et Kurt Jooss, qui émigrèrent en Angleterre en 1933 et s'installèrent à Dartington Hall.

'Down in the forest something stirred...' A group of German women dancers take to the great outdoors, 1935. Although she had died nearly 10 years earlier, the influence of Isadora Duncan was still enormously strong in Germany and Austria.

„Unten im Walde regte sich etwas ..." Eine Gruppe deutscher Tänzerinnen begeistert sich für die freie Natur, 1935. Selbst 10 Jahre nach ihrem Tod besaß Isadora Duncan noch immer einen sehr großen Einfluß in Deutschland und Österreich.

« Là-bas dans la forêt quelque chose remue... » Un groupe de danseuses allemandes s'épanouissent au grand air, 1935. Isadora Duncan était morte quelque 10 ans plus tôt mais son influence demeurait très grande en Allemagne et en Autriche.

August 1939. The war is less than a month away, but a group of well-drilled chorus girls go through their paces. In an age clattering with high-kicking precision routines, the Rockettes from Radio City Music Hall, New York, were reckoned the best.

August 1939. Bis zum Ausbruch des Krieges sollten nur noch vier Wochen vergehen, doch eine Truppe gut gedrillter Revuetänzerinnen probt wie gewohnt ihre Schrittfolgen. In dieser Zeit, als hoch in die Luft geworfene Beine allgegenwärtig schienen, galten die Rockettes der New Yorker Radio City Music Hall als die Besten.

Août 1939. La guerre éclatera dans un mois, mais ces danseuses bien entraînées font preuve de tout leur talent comme si de rien n'était. A une époque où tout devait rimer avec précision, les Rockettes du music-hall de Radio City étaient considérées comme les meilleures.

Sonia Hully, Yvonne Robinson and Bubbly Rogers in *Streamline* at the Palace Theatre, London, October 1934. They were three of impresario C B Cochran's renowned 'young ladies'. Noel Coward had many rows with 'Cockie' over the casting of stage-struck young women.

Sonia Hully, Yvonne Robinson und Bubbly Rogers in *Streamline* im Londoner Palace Theatre, Oktober 1934. Diese drei Damen gehörten zu Impresario C. B. Cochrans berühmten „young ladies". Noel Coward und „Cockie" hatten wiederholt Auseinandersetzungen über die Vergabe von Rollen an theaterbesessene junge Frauen.

Sonia Hully, Yvonne Robinson et Bubbly Rogers dans *Streamline* au Palace Theatre, Londres, octobre 1934. Elles faisaient partie des fameuses « jeunes demoiselles » engagées par l'imprésario C. B. Cochran. Noel Coward se disputa souvent avec « Cockie » à propos des filles qu'il choisissait et qui n'avaient qu'une envie, monter sur scène.

Three members of the chorus line of the Piccadilly Hotel cabaret, 1935. Almost every major hotel in London, Paris, New York or Berlin had its own band, cabaret, and dance floor in the Thirties.

Drei Revuemitglieder im Varieté des Piccadilly Hotels, 1935. Beinahe jedes große Hotel in London, Paris, New York oder Berlin hatte in den dreißiger Jahren seine eigene Tanzkapelle, ein Varieté und eine Tanzfläche.

Trois danseuses d'un spectacle au cabaret du Piccadilly Hôtel, 1935. Dans les années trente, presque chaque grand hôtel de Londres, Paris, New York ou Berlin avait son propre orchestre, son cabaret et sa piste de danse.

Members of the Margaret Morris Movement display their skills in a garden, 1935. Margaret Morris was a dance teacher who evolved her own techniques at the age of 17 and opened her first school two years later in 1910. The Movement combined medical and aesthetic values.

Mitglieder des Margaret Morris Movement stellen ihr Können zur Schau, 1935. Die Tanzlehrerin Margaret Morris entwickelte bereits im Alter von 17 Jahren, ihre eigene Tanztechnik und eröffnete zwei Jahre später im Jahre 1910 ihre erste Schule. Ihre Bewegung verband medizinische Aspekte mit ästhetischen Gesichtspunkten.

Des danseurs de la troupe Margaret Morris Movement exhibent leurs talents dans un jardin, 1935. Margaret Morris était professeur de danse. Elle développa sa propre technique à l'âge de 17 ans et ouvrit sa première école deux ans plus tard, en 1910. Son école associait des valeurs tant médicales qu'esthétiques.

Decidedly under the influence of Busby Berkeley, a circle of actresses seek an even suntan, 1935. They were members of the cast in a show called *Under the Palms*.

Unter dem unverwechselbaren Einfluß von Busby Berkeley bemüht sich eine Gruppe von Schauspielerinnen um eine gleichmäßige Sonnenbräune, 1935. Es handelt sich um Mitwirkende einer Show mit dem Titel *Unter den Palmen*.

Visiblement influencées par Busby Berkeley, ces actrices bronzent en cercle, 1935. Elles faisaient partie de la troupe d'un spectacle intitulé *Sous les palmiers*.

June 1937. Gracie Fields serenades workmen at the Prince of Wales Theatre, London. 'Our Gracie' had just laid the foundation stone of the new theatre. She was at the height of her popularity as a music-hall singer, comedienne and film star.

Juni 1937. Gracie Fields bringt Arbeitern im Londoner Prince of Wales Theatre ein Ständchen. „Unsere Gracie" hatte gerade den Grundstein des neuen Theaters gelegt und befand sich auf der Höhe ihrer Popularität als Varieté-Sängerin, Komödiantin und Filmstar.

Juin 1937. Gracie Fields répond en chantant à des ouvriers du Théâtre du Prince de Galles, Londres. « Notre Gracie » avait créé un nouveau genre théâtral. A la fois chanteuse de music-hall, comédienne et vedette de cinéma, elle était plus populaire que jamais.

September 1934.
Eric Gill at work on
*Christ Giving Sight
to Bartemus* for
the Moorfields Eye
Hospital, London.

September 1934.
Eric Gill bei der
Arbeit an *Christus
spendet Bartemus
das Augenlicht* für
das Moorfields Eye
Hospital in London.

Septembre 1934.
Eric Gill à l'œuvre
sur *Christ donna la
vue à Bartémus*
pour l'hôpital
ophtalmologique de
Moorfields, Londres.

Jacob Epstein, the American-born sculptor, at work in 1931 on *Genesis*, for which he was accused of both indecency and blasphemy.

Der gebürtige Amerikaner Jacob Epstein 1931 bei der Arbeit an der Skulptur *Genesis*, die ihm den Vorwurf der Anstößigkeit und der Blasphemie einbrachte.

Jacob Epstein, sculpteur d'origine américaine, en 1931 aux côtés de *Genèse* qui lui valut d'être accusé d'outrage aux bonnes mœurs et de blasphème.

July 1938. Adolf Hitler (fourth from left) with Joseph Goebbels at the Nazi 'Day of Art' Exhibition in Munich. The exhibition included a five-mile (eight-kilometre) parade representing 2,000 years of German culture.

Juli 1938. Adolf Hitler (vierter von links) und Joseph Goebbels in der Münchener Propaganda-Ausstellung „Tag der Kunst". Anläßlich der Ausstellung fand auch eine acht Kilometer lange Parade statt, die 2.000 Jahre deutscher Kultur vor Augen führen sollte.

Juillet 1938. Adolf Hitler (quatrième à partir de la gauche) accompagné de Goebbels lors de l'inauguration de l'exposition nazie « Journée de l'Art » à Munich. Cette exposition comprenait un défilé long de huit kilomètres mettant en scène deux millénaires de culture allemande.

July 1938. Max Beckmann's triptych, *Temptation*, goes on show at the new Burlington Galleries, London. It was part of an exhibition of the work of German artists who had been labelled 'degenerate' by Hitler, and was staged in rivalry to the Nazi Exhibition in Munich.

Juli 1938. Max Beckmanns Triptychon *Versuchung* in den neuen Burlington Galleries in London. Es war teil einer Ausstellung über deutsche „entartete" Kunst – eine Konkurrenz-Veranstaltung zur Münchener Nazi-Ausstellung.

Juillet 1938. Installation du triptyque *Tentation* de Max Beckmann aux nouvelles Galeries de Burlington à Londres. Ce tableau et d'autres œuvres d'artistes allemands qu'Hitler avait traités de « dégénérés » faisaient partie d'une exposition montée en réponse à celle des nazis à Munich.

May 1939. Walter Gropius (left) with his wife, Ise Frank, and the French architect Le Corbusier at a Paris café. In 1919 Gropius founded the famous Bauhaus art school, which was closed by Hitler in 1933. Gropius and his wife fled first to Britain, then to the United States.

Mai 1939. Walter Gropius (links) mit seiner Ehefrau, Ise Frank, und dem französischen Architekten Le Corbusier in einem Pariser Café. Gropius hatte 1919 das Bauhaus gegründet, das 1933 durch die Nationalsozialisten geschlossen wurde. Er floh mit seiner Ehefrau zunächst nach Großbritannien und später in die Vereinigten Staaten.

Mai 1939. Walter Gropius (à gauche) avec sa femme, Ise Frank, et l'architecte français Le Corbusier dans un café à Paris. En 1919 Gropius fonda le Bauhaus, célèbre école d'architecture et d'art fermée par Hitler en 1933. Gropius et sa femme émigrèrent d'abord en Grande-Bretagne puis aux Etats-Unis.

August 1939. Irish-born dramatist George Bernard Shaw outside the German embassy in London. A tough month lay ahead for pacifists as Europe hastened to war.

August 1939. Der gebürtige Ire George Bernard Shaw vor der deutschen Botschaft in London. Als Europa sich in den Krieg stürzte, stand Pazifisten ein harter Monat bevor.

Août 1939. Le dramaturge irlandais George Bernard Shaw devant l'Ambassade d'Allemagne à Londres. Le mois s'annonçait mouvementé pour les pacifistes, alors que l'Europe se précipitait dans la guerre.

Soviet novelist and
playwright Maxim
Gorky, 1932.
He died four years
later, in mysterious
circumstances,
while under medical
treatment.

Der sowjetische
Schriftsteller und
Dramatiker Maxim
Gorki, 1932. Vier
Jahre später starb er
unter ungeklärten
Umständen, obwohl
er sich in ärztlicher
Behandlung befand.

L'écrivain et
dramaturge
soviétique Maxime
Gorki, 1932. Il
mourut quatre ans
plus tard dans des
circonstances
mystérieuses alors
qu'il suivait un
traitement médical.

Leon Trotsky working on his *History of the Russian Revolution* in 1931. He had been banished from the Soviet Union in 1929. This picture was taken in his study at Principe in the Gulf of Guinea.

Leo Trotzkij arbeitet 1931 an seiner *Geschichte der russischen Revolution*. Zwei Jahre zuvor war er aus der Sowjetunion ausgewiesen worden. Diese Aufnahme entstand in seinem Arbeitszimmer in Principe im Golf von Guinea.

Léon Trotski travaillant sur son *Histoire de la révolution russe* en 1931. Il fut expulsé d'Union soviétique en 1929. Cette photographie fut prise dans son étude à Principe dans le golfe de Guinée.

A Hollywood lunch, April 1933. (From left to right) Charlie Chaplin, George Bernard Shaw, Marion Davies, Louis B Mayer, Clark Gable and George Hearst. Shaw had been touring the States, and had given a lecture on political economy in New York. Maybe that was also the trouble here.

Ein Mittagessen in Hollywood, April 1933. (Von links nach rechts) Charlie Chaplin, George Bernard Shaw, Marion Davies, Louis B. Mayer, Clark Gable und George Hearst. Shaw hatte die Vereinigten Staaten bereist und in New York einen Vortrag über Volkswirtschaft gehalten, der auch hier der Grund für die Beunruhigung sein mag.

Déjeuner à Hollywood, avril 1933. (De gauche à droite) Charlie Chaplin, George Bernard Shaw, Marion Davies, Louis B. Mayer, Clark Gable et George Hearst. En visite aux Etats-Unis, Shaw venait de donner une conférence d'économie politique à New York et ici aussi peut-être, à voir le sérieux affiché par les convives.

Lady Trowbridge (left) and Radclyffe Hall attend the first night of the
appropriately named *When Ladies Meet* at the Lyric Theatre in London,
1933. Radclyffe Hall's open lesbianism shocked Thirties society.

Lady Trowbridge (links) und Radclyffe Hall bei der Premiere des
passend betitelten Stückes *Wenn Frauen sich treffen* im Londoner Lyric
Theatre, 1933. Die Lesbierin Radclyffe Halls die ihre Neigung
unverhohlen auslebte, schockierte die Gesellschaft der dreißiger Jahre.

Lady Trowbridge (à gauche) et Radclyffe Hall à la première du spectacle,
bien nommé en l'occurrence, *Quand les femmes se rencontrent* au
Théâtre lyrique de Londres, 1933. L'attitude ouvertement lesbienne de
Radclyffe Hall choqua la société des années trente.

7. Fashion
Mode
La mode

A 1934 fashion plate by Nicolet. The woman is wearing *gants de trill* and lace cuffs. Accessories such as gloves, bags, shoes and a little jewellery were of the utmost importance for the well-dressed woman in the Thirties.

Eine Modeaufnahme von Nicolet, 1934. Das Mannequin führt Tüllhandschuhe und Spitzenmanschetten vor. Accessoires wie Handschuhe, Handtaschen, Schuhe und ein wenig Schmuck waren für die modebewußte Frau in den dreißiger Jahren unentbehrlich.

Figure de mode par Nicolet, 1934. Le mannequin porte des gants de tulle parés de dentelle. Les accessoires – gants, sacs, chaussures et quelques bijoux – étaient absolument essentiels à la femme élégante des années trente.

7. Fashion
Mode
La mode

The most colourful excesses of the Twenties disappeared – no college freshman would have been seen dead in a raccoon coat. Skirts crept down the leg – a well-dressed mobster like Bonnie Parker showed the merest glimpse of lower calf. Waists were nipped in, chests flat, dresses long and elegant. Slacks were bold, loose and comfortable. Hair was worn longer – the page-boy bobs of the Twenties now grew into long and lustrous tresses.

Apart from the introduction of the Windsor knot for neckwear, men's fashion hardly changed. For the well-off there was an increasing emphasis on top hat, white tie and tails, but an unemployed miner or farm hand looked little different from his unemployed grandfather.

Hats for women were snug-fitting, adorable, provocative. One look at Bette Davis in a beret or that sweet pill-box she wore in *Special Agent* and tears sprang to the eyes. For something sexier, there was nothing to beat the feather-faced gown that Ginger Rogers wore when she danced cheek to cheek with Fred in *Top Hat*, even though it got up his nose.

Paris called all the fashion shots: the rest of the world was nowhere. Fur, on the other hand, was everywhere – in those days nobody cared where it came from – on collars, hats, gloves, stoles, and cuffs. And nylon made a late entry in 1939, promising elegance for the masses.

Die schillernden Ausschweifungen der zwanziger Jahre verschwanden eine Dekade später. Kein angehender Student hätte sich nunmehr in einem Mantel aus Waschbärfell in der Öffentlichkeit gezeigt. Der Rocksaum wanderte nach unten, die Taille war eng, der Busen flach und die Kleider flossen lang und elegant. Lange Hosen waren weit und bequem geschnitten. Das Haar wurde wieder länger, so daß sich die Pagenköpfe der zwanziger Jahre in lange, verführerische Locken verwandelten.

Die Herrenmode änderte sich – abgesehen von der Einführung des Windsor-Krawattenknotens – kaum. In gehobenen Kreisen legte man zunehmend Wert auf Zylinder und Frack-schöße, doch ein arbeitsloser Bergmann oder Landarbeiter unterschied sich rein äußerlich kaum von seinem arbeitslosen Großvater.

Die hinreißenden Damenhüte waren klein und provokativ. Nur ein Blick auf Bette Davis mit Baskenmütze oder jener Pillbox, die sie in *Spezialagent* trug, und man schmolz dahin. Was den verführerischen Look anging, war allerdings das federnbesetzte Abendkleid von Ginger Rogers konkurrenzlos, in dem sie Wange an Wange mit Fred Astaire in *Top Hat* tanzte – selbst wenn es ihn an der Nase kitzelte.

Paris avancierte zum unumstrittenen Zentrum der Mode. Unverzichtbar waren Pelze, und in jenen Tagen kümmerte sich niemand darum, woher sie stammten: Man fand sie an Kragen, Hüten und Handschuhen, an Stolen und Manschetten. Nylon hatte schließlich einen späten Auftritt im Jahre 1939 und versprach endlich Eleganz für jedermann.

Les excès flamboyants des années folles disparurent. Pas un étudiant n'aurait porté, même mort, un manteau en raton laveur. Les jupes s'allongèrent et une gangster aussi élégante que Bonnie Parker n'aurait jamais laissé entrevoir son mollet. La taille était pincée, la poitrine plate, les robes longues et chics. Les pantalons étaient amples et confortables avec des motifs originaux. Les cheveux se portaient plus longs, en longues et superbes nattes – fini le carré court des années vingt.

Hormis le nouveau nœud Windsor au rayon des cravates, la mode pour hommes ne changea guère. Pour ceux qui en avaient les moyens, le haut-de-forme, l'habit et le queue-de-pie étaient de plus en plus convoités. Quant au sans-emploi ou à l'ouvrier agricole, il était vêtu à peu près comme son grand-père chômeur.

Les chapeaux de femme, adorables et provocants, se portaient bien ajustés. Bette Davis, coiffée de son béret ou de la toque qu'elle avait dans *Agent spécial*, est irrésistible. Dans un registre plus sexy, rien n'égalait la robe à plumes portée par Ginger Rogers pour danser joue contre joue avec Fred, *Le danseur du dessus*. Tant pis si les plumes le faisaient éternuer.

Paris était la capitale de la mode. La fourrure devint un accessoire de base qui ornait cols, chapeaux, gants, étoles et manches – peu importe de quel animal elle provenait. Le nylon arriva plus tard, en 1939, promettant aux masses une élégance future.

August 1934. Low-backed cheek. Two young couples stroll along
the promenade at Thorpe Bay, Essex. At the seaside, more flesh was
visible than ever before, though swimsuits were still in one piece.

August 1934. Gewagte Rückenansicht. Zwei junge Pärchen
schlendern über die Promenade von Thorpe Bay in Essex.
Am Meer gab man sich offenherziger als je zuvor, obwohl die
Badebekleidung auch weiterhin einteilig blieb.

Août 1934. Dos nus. Jeunes couples en promenade le long de la
Baie de Thorpe, Essex. Au bord de la mer, on se découvrait de plus
en plus, mais les maillots de bain étaient encore des une-pièce.

High-hat chic.
Mrs Meade (left)
and Mrs McClure,
heading for Ascot in
1936, make the
mistake of wearing
almost identical fur
jackets.

Blasierter Schick.
Mrs. Meade (links)
und Mrs. McClure
begehen den Fehler,
beim Besuch der
Pferderennen von
Ascot nahezu
identische Pelzjacken
zu tragen, 1936.

Elégance aristo-
cratique, Ascot,
1936. Mme Meade
(à gauche) et Mme
McClure font
l'impair de porter
des vestes en
fourrure presque
identiques.

June 1932.
Wide-legged trousers
and bold graphic
prints mark the
Nichols of Regent
Street show in
London.

Juni 1932.
Weit geschnittene
Hosen und kühne
grafische Muster
sind das besondere
Merkmal der
Modenschau von
Nichols of Regent
Street in London.

Juin 1932.
Pantalons amples
et motifs osés
marquent la
collection présentée
par Nichols de
Regent Street à
Londres.

June 1939.
Muriel Oxford
displays the 'boating
shorts' worn beneath
a wraparound skirt.

Juni 1939.
Muriel Oxford
präsentiert ein Paar
„Shorts für die
Bootsfahrt", die
unter einem Rock
getragen werden.

Juin 1939.
Muriel Oxford vêtue
d'un « short-bateau »
qui se porte sous une
jupe-portefeuille.

June 1938. Women bowlers at the Stanley Park club in Blackpool. Blackpool
was at the height of its popularity as a seaside resort, and was 'noted for fresh air
and fun'. The slacks worn by the woman about to play are typical of the time.

Juni 1938. Vier Damen beim Bowling im Blackpooler Stanley Park Club.
Blackpool war damals das beliebteste Seebad überhaupt und für „Frischluft und
Freude" bekannt. Die Spielerin, die gerade wirft, trägt eine für jene Zeit typische
Hose.

Juin 1938. Joueuses de boules au club de Stanley Park à Blackpool. Blackpool
était une station balnéaire plus cotée que jamais, « appréciée pour son air frais et
ses divertissements ». Les pantalons de la femme qui s'apprête à jouer sont
typiques de l'époque.

Mrs D Alusarez demonstrates the benefits of a divided skirt for women players at the North London Tennis Tournament, Highbury, London, in 1931. Her partner (or opponent) appears transfixed.

Mrs. D. Alusarez demonstriert die Vorteile eines Hosenrocks bei einem Tennisturnier in Highbury, Nord-London, 1931. Ihre Partnerin (oder Gegnerin) scheint allerdings nicht sehr begeistert zu sein.

Concours de tennis du nord de Londres à Highbury, 1931. Mme D. Alusarez montre les avantages de la jupe-pantalon pour une joueuse de tennis. Sa partenaire (ou son adversaire) en demeure ébahie.

A man faces the gaze of hundreds as he models beachwear on an open-air catwalk, 1935. The photograph is all the more remarkable in that it was taken in England – not at that time a country associated with fashion design, fine weather or male models.

Ein männliches Model stellt sich 1935 Hunderten von Zuschauern und führt unter freiem Himmel Strandmode bei einer Modenschau vor. Die Aufnahme ist um so bemerkenswerter, als England zu jener Zeit weder mit Mode, noch mit Dressmen oder mit schönem Wetter in Verbindung gebracht wurde.

Un homme, sous le regard de la foule, défile en maillot de bain sur une estrade montée en plein air, 1935. Ce cliché est surprenant car il a été pris en Angleterre alors guère connue pour sa mode, son beau temps ou ses mannequins hommes.

The American film
actress Frances
Drake shows off her
high-waisted slacks
as she walks through
the Paramount lot,
1934.

Die amerikanische
Filmschauspielerin
Frances Drake zeigt
stolz ihre hoch
geschnittene Hose
auf dem Gelände der
Paramount Studios,
1934.

L'actrice américaine
Frances Drake
arbore fièrement ses
pantalons à taille
haute sur le terrain
des studios
Paramount, 1934.

May 1933. Six of the Busby Berkeley babes from *Gold Diggers of 1933* parade outside the Warner Brothers Studio, Hollywood. The publicity material for the film boasted, 'Your dreams of perfect beauty come true!' The photographer clearly chose his lighting with great care.

Mai 1933. Sechs von Busby Berkeley geschulte Tänzerinnen aus dem Film *Goldgräber von 1933* posieren vor dem Studio der Warner Brothers in Hollywood. Die Filmwerbung prahlte: „Ihr Traum von vollkommener Schönheit wird wahr!" Der Fotograf achtete jedenfalls bei dieser Aufnahme sehr sorgfältig auf die Lichtverhältnisse.

Mai 1933. Six des *Chercheuses d'or* de 1933 de Busby Berkeley prennent la pose à l'extérieur des studios de la Warner, Hollywood. « La beauté de vos rêves existe enfin ! » proclamait la publicité du film. Quant au photographe, il prit soin de choisir le bon angle.

Lillian Harvey, 1932. Harvey was born in England, became a German film star, and then moved to Hollywood. She was known as 'the sweetest girl in the world'.

Lillian Harvey, 1932. Die gebürtige Engländerin, die in Deutschland zum Filmstar wurde, siedelte später nach Hollywood über. Man nannte sie „das süßeste Mädchen der Welt".

Lillian Harvey, 1932. Née en Angleterre, Harvey devint une vedette en Allemagne avant d'émigrer à Hollywood. Elle passait pour être « la fille la plus gentille au monde ».

Elsa Schiaparelli (right) in Hyde Park, London, 1930. Schiaparelli was the fashion designer who pioneered 'Trousers for Women'.

Die Modeschöpferin Elsa Schiaparelli (rechts) 1930 im Londoner Hyde Park. Sie leistete Pionierarbeit auf dem Gebiet „Hosen für Frauen".

La styliste Elsa Schiaparelli (à droite) à Hyde Park, Londres, 1930. Ce fut elle qui lança le slogan « des pantalons pour les femmes ».

Amy Johnson wears
a woollen suit
designed for her by
Schiaparelli after
Johnson had flown
solo from London to
Cape Town, 1936.

Die Fliegerin Amy
Johnson trägt ein
Wollkostüm, das
Elsa Schiaparelli für
sie entwarf,
nachdem Johnson
1936 im Alleinflug
die Strecke London
– Kapstadt bewältigt
hatte.

Amy Johnson porte
un ensemble en laine
créé pour elle par
Schiaparelli après
son vol en solitaire
de Londres au Cap,
1936.

Taking the message abroad. A Parisian model wears Union Jack stockings at
an open-air café, June 1938. She was almost certainly greeted with more
warmth than English football fans wearing Union Jack T-shirts 60 years later.

Englischer Patriotismus im Ausland. Ein Model trägt in einem Pariser
Straßencafé Strümpfe, die die britische Flagge ziert, Juni 1938. Wahr-
scheinlich wurde sie herzlicher empfangen, als 60 Jahre später englische
Fußballfans in T-Shirts mit dem gleichen Emblem.

Porte-drapeau. Mannequin parisien, parée de bas aux couleurs britanniques,
à la terrasse d'un café, juin 1938. Elle fut probablement accueillie avec
plus d'enthousiasme que les supporters de football anglais vêtus de T-shirts
arborant le même drapeau 60 ans plus tard.

August 1939. Phyllis Gordon goes window shopping in London,
with her four-year-old cheetah who was flown to Britain from
Kenya. Very little time remained before clothes became rationed.

August 1939. Phyllis Gordon und ihr vierjähriger Gepard,
der aus Kenia eingeflogen worden ist, bei einem Schaufenster-
bummel in London. Es sollte nicht mehr lange dauern,
bis Kleidung rationiert wurde.

Août 1939. Phyllis Gordon fait du lèche-vitrine à Londres en
compagnie de son guépard, âgé de quatre ans qu'elle avait
ramené du Kenya par avion. Peu de temps après, les vêtements
seraient rationnés.

British dancer
Rosemary Andrée on
a summer's day at
Roehampton Pool,
London, June 1939.
It's one way of
making sure you can
meet under the
clock.

Die britische
Tänzerin Rosemary
Andrée verbringt
einen schönen
Sommertag im
Schwimmbad von
Roehampton,
London, Juni 1939.
Dies ist sicherlich
eine Möglichkeit für
ein Rendez-vous
unter der großen
Uhr.

La danseuse
britannique
Rosemary Andrée à
la piscine de
Roehampton,
Londres, juin 1939.
Chapeau idéal pour
un premier rendez-
vous sous l'horloge.

1936. A patriotic
parade in Hastings,
on the south coast of
England.

1936. Patriotismus
in Hastings, an der
Südküste Englands.

1936. Promenade
patriotique à
Hastings, sur la côte
sud de l'Angleterre.

December 1938. A woman fastens her stockings as she prepares to dress
for lunch. The pose is classic, and lightly titillating. From the look of the
dress on the stand, the stockings were more likely to be silk than nylon.

Dezember 1938. Eine Dame zieht sich in klassischer Pose zum Essen um.
Nach dem Kleid auf dem Ständer zu urteilen, trägt sie wohl eher
Seidenstrümpfe als solche aus Nylon.

Décembre 1938. Séance d'habillage avant le déjeuner. La pose est
classique et légèrement provocante. A voir la robe exposée, il est presque
sûr que les bas que porte cette femme sont en soie et pas en nylon.

A window display of Scandale corsets, 1935. Foundation garments were
still much in demand. It would take the liberating experience of a
World War II war before women were happy to manage without support.

Ein mit Korsetts der Marke Scandale dekoriertes Schaufenster im Jahre
1935, als Mieder noch sehr begehrt waren. Erst nach dem Zweiten
Weltkrieg sollten sich die Frauen von Mieder und Korsett befreien.

Vitrine exposant les gaines Scandale, 1935. Les gaines étaient toujours
très en vogue. Après la Seconde Guerre mondiale, les femmes libérèrent
davantage leur corps et portèrent des dessous plus simples.

8. Science
Wissenschaft
La science

July 1932. A brilliant young scientist claims to have invented the world's most 'perfect' robot. The cost was £6,000, but for that you got a machine that could talk, sing, whistle ('for 30 minutes'), carry on a conversation, tell the time of day, read a newspaper and fire a revolver.

Juli 1932. Ein brillanter junger Wissenschaftler behauptet, den „perfekten" Roboter erfunden zu haben. Er kostete stattliche 6.000 Pfund, aber dafür konnte er sprechen, singen, pfeifen (30 Minuten lang), sich unterhalten, die Uhrzeit ansagen, eine Zeitung lesen und mit einem Revolver schießen.

Juillet 1932. Un jeune et brillant scientifique déclare avoir inventé le robot le plus perfectionné du monde. Pour £ 6 000, vous aviez une machine qui savait parler, chanter, siffler (pendant 30 minutes), faire la conversation, donner l'heure, lire le journal et se servir d'une arme.

8. Science
Wissenschaft
La science

The image of Thirties science is one of laboratories crammed with resistors and rheostats, flashing bulbs and humming valves, and festooned with long coils of wire and strands of flex. It's the age of movies like *Frankenstein* and *The Invisible Man*, of eccentric inventors in workshops as cluttered as the inside of the human body.

But it was also the decade that saw the completion of the world's tallest building and the world's most beautiful bridges, the beginnings of television services, the invention of nylon and cellophane, the coming of age of radar and the rocket, and the splitting of the atom.

Most research into science or technology was devoted to projects that had a military use. The rush was on to create planes that could fly greater distances, faster and more reliably, simply because those would be the ones to win a war. Tyres were tougher, trucks more powerful, weapons deadlier than ever. Igor Sikorsky, a Russian-born aeronautical engineer, made the prototype helicopter in 1939, and George G Blaisdell invented the wind-proof Zippo cigarette lighter in 1932.

The public were delighted by all these developments – for the time being.

Unser Bild von der Wissenschaft der dreißiger Jahre wird von chaotischen Labors, voll von Widerständen, Blitzbirnen, dem Gewirr langer Drahtspiralen und Kabelschnüre geprägt. Es ist die Epoche von Filmen wie *Frankenstein* und *Der Unsichtbare Mann*, von exzentrischen Erfindern inmitten ihrer chaotischen Laboratorien wie im Innern menschlicher Körper.

In Wirklichkeit war es ganz anders, denn in jener Zeit entstanden das höchste Gebäude der Welt und die besten Brückenkonstruktionen. Wissenschaftler schufen ein Betriebsnetz für das Fernsehen, entwickelten die Stoffe Nylon und Cellophan, perfektionierten das Radar und die Rakete und spalteten den Atomkern.

Der größte Teil der Forschung in Wissenschaft und Technologie war jedoch militärischen Projekten gewidmet. Es sollten Flugzeuge entwickelt werden, die größere Entfernungen zurücklegen konnten und dabei schneller und zuverlässiger waren – einfach aus dem Grund, weil man mit ihnen einen Krieg gewinnen wollte. Autoreifen waren nun widerstandsfähiger, Lastkraftwagen antriebsstärker und Waffen tödlicher als je zuvor. Der gebürtige Russe und Flugzeugingenieur Igor Sikorsky entwickelte im Jahre 1939 den Prototyp eines Helikopters, und George G. Blaisdell erfand 1932 das Sturmfeuerzeug.

Die Bevölkerung war von all diesen Entwicklungen begeistert – jedenfalls vorläufig.

L'image de la science dans les années trente est celle d'un laboratoire rempli de conducteurs de résistance et de rhéostats, d'ampoules clignotantes et de soupapes vrombissantes, traversé de câbles et de fils électriques. C'est l'époque des films comme *Frankenstein* ou *L'homme invisible* et, inventeurs excentriques au milieu de laboratoires de fortune aussi encombrés que l'intérieur du corps humain.

Mais ce fut aussi la décennie qui assista à la construction de la plus haute tour et des plus beaux ponts du monde, aux débuts de la télévision, à l'invention du nylon et du cellophane, au perfectionnement des radars et des missiles et à la fission de l'atome.

La plupart des recherches scientifiques ou technologiques avaient des fins militaires. Il y avait urgence à créer des avions qui pourraient voler plus loin, plus vite et plus sûrement, tout simplement parce que de tels avions permettraient de gagner la guerre. Les pneus étaient plus solides, les camions plus puissants et les armes plus meurtrières que jamais. En 1939, Igor Sikorsky, un ingénieur en aéronautique d'origine russe, réalisa le premier prototype d'hélicoptère et, en 1932, George G. Blaisdell inventa le Zippo, le premier briquet à résister au vent.

Le public était admiratif devant tant de progrès, du moins pour l'instant.

January 1932. Opening up world communication
– part of the General Post Office exhibition of telephones
at the Imperial Institute, Kensington, London.

Januar 1932. Die Anfänge weltweiter Kommunikation –
ein Stand auf der Telefonausstellung des Hauptpostamtes
im Imperial Institute in Kensington, London.

Janvier 1932. Début des communications à l'échelle
mondiale – stand d'une exposition sur les téléphones
de la Poste à l'Institut impérial, Kensington, Londres.

Members of the
German police force
use two-way radios
to send and receive
messages from
patrols, 1935.

Deutsche Polizei-
beamte setze Funk-
sprechgeräte ein,
um mit Streifen-
polizisten kommu-
nizieren zu können,
1935.

Des policiers
allemands utilisent
un émetteur-
récepteur pour
envoyer et recevoir
des messages entre
patrouilles, 1935.

1932. The Swiss
physicist, Auguste
Piccard, enters his
balloon before the
start of his successful
attempt on the
world's altitude
record.

1932. Der schweizer
Physiker Auguste
Piccard steigt in
seinen Fesselballon,
mit dem er einen
neuen Weltrekord
im Höhenflug
aufstellte.

1932. Le physicien
suisse, Auguste
Piccard, prend place
dans son ballon qui
lui permit de battre
le record du monde
d'altitude.

February 1932.
The 'dynosphere',
an electrically driven
wheel, is tested on
the beach at Weston-
super-Mare by one
of its two inventors.

Februar 1932.
Einer der beiden
Erfinder der
„Dynosphäre" testet
dieses elektrisch
angetriebene Rad am
Strand von Weston-
super-Mare.

Février 1932.
La dynosphère, une
roue à moteur
électrique, est
essayée par l'un de
ses deux inventeurs
sur la plage de
Weston-super-Mare.

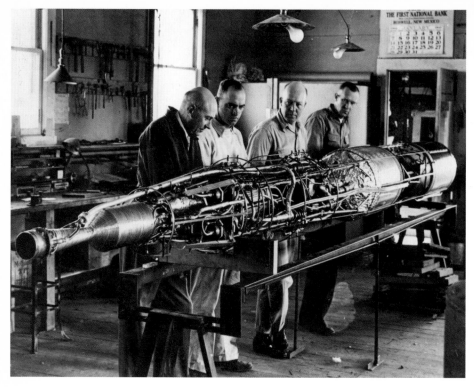

The rocket pioneer, Dr Robert Hutchinge Goddard (left) works
with three of his colleagues on a prototype rocket. The casing has been
removed, and the sophistication of Thirties science is clear to see.

Der Raketenpionier Dr. Robert Hutchinge Goddard (links) arbeitet
mit drei Kollegen am Prototyp einer Rakete. Da das Gehäuse entfernt
worden ist, kann man den hohen Entwicklungsstand der Wissenschaft
in den dreißiger Jahren deutlich erkennen.

Le Dr. Robert Hutchinge Goddard (à gauche), pionnier du missile,
travaille avec trois collègues sur un prototype. Le système ainsi mis
à nu permet de voir la sophistication de la science de cette époque.

The fastest car in the world, 1932. The model is an Opel, powered by 24 rockets in the tail end. It was designed by Fritz von Opel, and was first successfully driven in Berlin.

Das schnellste Auto der Welt, 1932. Fritz von Opel entwickelte dieses von 24 Raketen angetriebene Modell, das seine erste erfolgreiche Fahrt in Berlin absolvierte.

Une des voitures les plus rapides du monde, 1932. Ce modèle, propulsé par 24 fusées placées à l'arrière du véhicule, fut conçu par Fritz von Opel et testé avec succès pour la première fois à Berlin.

A television set at
the Radio Olympia
Exhibition, London,
1939. Sets like these
were expected to be
available to the
public in 1960.

Ein Fernseher in
der Radio Olympia
Exhibition in
London, 1939.
Man ging davon aus,
daß solche Geräte
1960 im Handel sein
würden.

Poste de télévision
installé à l'exposition
de Radio Olympia,
Londres, 1939.
Il était prévu que ces
appareils seraient
accessibles au public
en 1960.

Mr Grindell Matthews with his photographic gun, 1933. The gun could project a beam of light 15 miles (24 kilometres) into the sky.

Mr. Grindell Matthews und seine Fotokanone, 1933. Dieses monströse Gerät konnte einen Lichtstrahl 24 Kilometer weit in den Himmel projizieren.

M. Grindell Matthews et son canon photographique, 1933. Ce canon pouvait projeter dans le ciel un faisceau lumineux long de 24 kilomètres.

May 1939. Children from Bradford line up for a dose of medicine
while on holiday in Morecambe, Lancashire. The drive for
better public health accelerated towards the end of the Thirties.

Mai 1939. Kinder aus Bradford erhalten während der Ferien
in Morecambe, Lancashire, ihren Löffel Medizin. In den späten
dreißiger Jahren bemühte man sich sehr darum, die Gesundheit
der Bevölkerung zu verbessern.

Mai 1939. Des enfants de Bradford en vacances à Morecambe,
Lancashire, font la queue pour prendre un médicament.
La campagne en faveur d'une meilleure santé publique s'accéléra
vers la fin des années trente.

Members of the
Arsenal football
team get their daily
anti-influenza
treatment during the
epidemic of 1937.

Während der
Grippewelle von
1937 erhalten die
Spieler des
Fußballvereins
Arsenal täglich
neuen Grippeschutz.

Traitement
antigrippe quotidien
pour les joueurs du
club de football
d'Arsenal durant
l'épidémie de 1937.

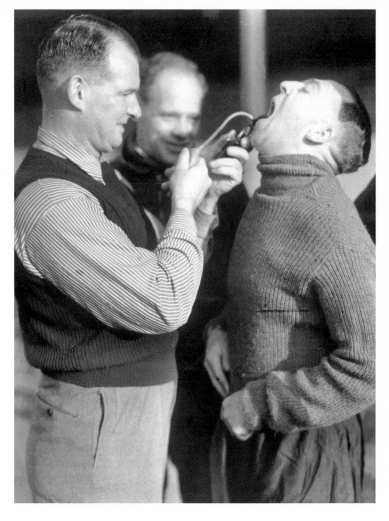

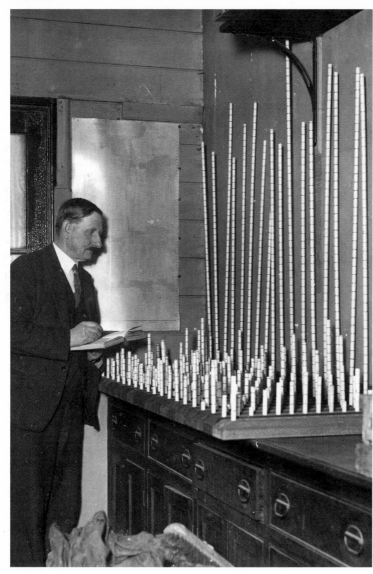

April 1932.
Mr Lock's unique
system of recording
the rainfall over 18
years. The short rods
record the monthly
fall, the long rods
the annual fall.

April 1932. Mr.
Locks einzigartige
Statistik der Nieder-
schläge der ver-
gangenen 18 Jahre.
Die kurzen Stäbe
verdeutlichen den
monatlichen Nieder-
schlag, die langen
den jährlichen.

Avril 1932.
Ce système unique,
conçu par M. Lock,
permit d'enregistrer
le taux de pluviosité
pendant 18 ans. Les
petites baguettes
indiquent les chutes
de pluie mensuelles,
les grandes, les
chutes annuelles.

London 1935.
One of the first of
the Belisha beacons
being installed in
Hanwell Broadway.
The beacons, named
after the 1934
minister of
transport, flashed at
night, and marked
pedestrian crossings.

London 1935.
Am Hanwell
Broadway wird eines
der ersten Belisha-
Leuchtsignale
installiert. Diese
Blinksignale, die
nachts auf Fuß-
gängerüberwege
aufmerksam
machten, wurden
nach dem Verkehrs-
minister des Jahres
1934 benannt.

Londres, 1935.
Installation sur
Hanwell Broadway
de l'un des premiers
lampadaires baptisés
Belisha, d'après le
nom du Ministre des
Transports de 1934.
Ils signalaient les
passages cloutés et
clignotaient la nuit.

1930. Crowds swarm across Sydney Harbour Bridge on their
way to the official opening ceremony. For many years the bridge
was a national symbol, and the pride of all Australians.

1930. Tausende von Menschen strömen zur offiziellen
Eröffnungszeremonie der Hafenbrücke von Sydney. Die Brücke
war der Stolz der australischen Bevölkerung und wurde noch
viele Jahre lang als Symbol des Landes betrachtet.

1930. La foule envahit le pont du port de Sidney pour se rendre
à la cérémonie d'inauguration officielle. Ce pont fut longtemps
un symbole national et un objet de fierté pour les Australiens.

The Golden Gate
Bridge, San
Francisco, 1938
– a year after
completion. It had
a span of 4,200 feet
(1,300 metres), the
longest in the world.

Die Golden Gate
Bridge in San
Francisco, 1938, ein
Jahr nach ihrer
Fertigstellung. Mit
ihrer Spannweite
von 1.300 Metern
war sie die längste
Brücke der Welt.

Le pont du Golden
Gate, San Francisco,
1938 – un an après
son achèvement.
Avec une portée de
1 300 mètres, c'était
le pont le plus long
du monde.

London, 1930.
The ornate interior
of the New Victoria
cinema. Picture
'palaces' were rightly
named.

London, 1930.
Die aufwendige
Art-Deco-Innen-
ausstattung des
Kinos New Victoria.
Zu Recht be-
zeichnete man diese
Kinos als „Film-
paläste".

Londres, 1930.
Le décor très orné
de la salle du New
Victoria. Les
cinémas portaient
des noms de
« palais », à juste
titre.

Part of the North London Exhibition at Alexandra Palace, 1932.
The house is a typical Thirties 'semi-detached', built in hundreds
of thousands in the suburbs on the outskirts of British cities.

Auf der North-London-Messe im Alexandra Palau, 1932. Diese
Doppelhaushälfte ist typisch für die dreißiger Jahre. Sie wurden
zu Hundertausenden in den Vororten britischer Städte gebaut.

A la foire du Nord de Londres, Alexandra Palace, 1932. Voici
une maison mitoyenne typique des années trente, comme il en
fut construit des centaines de milliers dans les banlieues des
villes britanniques.

An aerial view of
the Empire State
Building, New York,
1935. There were
also plans to build a
landing mast on top
for airships.

Die Luftaufnahme
zeigt das Empire
State Building in
New York, 1935.
Für die Spitze des
Wolkenkratzers war
ein Landemast zur
Verankerung von
Luftschiffen
vorgesehen.

Vue aérienne de
l'Empire State
Building, New York,
1935. Il avait été
question de
construire sur le
sommet une aire
d'atterrissage pour
les dirigeables.

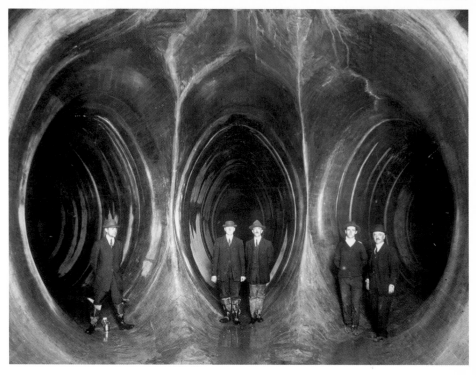

1935. The meeting point of three tunnels in New York's Catskill aqueduct. In the mid-Thirties the population of the city reached 6.4 million, and providing the essential services was a problem for the newly elected mayor, Fiorello LaGuardia.

1935. Die Nahtstelle dreier Tunnel im New Yorker Abwasserkanalsystem Catskill. Mitte der dreißiger Jahre wuchs die Einwohnerzahl der Stadt auf 6,4 Millionen an. Dementsprechend mußte der neugewählte Bürgermeister Fiorello LaGuardia das städtische Versorgungsnetz anpassen.

1935. Point de rencontre des trois tunnels de l'aqueduc de Catskill à New York. Au milieu des années trente, la ville atteint les 6,4 millions d'habitants, posant au maire nouvellement élu, Fiorello LaGuardia, le problème des services essentiels à assurer.

9. Transport
Verkehrswesen
Moyens de transport

The German experimental locomotive *Railway Zeppelin*, May 1931. Although it was planned to run along conventional tracks, it was powered from the rear by a large four-bladed propeller.

Die deutsche Versuchslokomotive „Eisenbahn-Zeppelin", Mai 1931. Obwohl geplant war, die Lok auf herkömmlichen Schienen einzusetzen, wurde sie von einem großen, vierflügeligen Propeller angetrieben.

Une locomotive expérimentale allemande en forme de zeppelin, mai 1931. Conçue pour rouler sur des rails conventionnels, elle était néanmoins propulsée par une énorme hélice à quatre pales, placée à l'arrière.

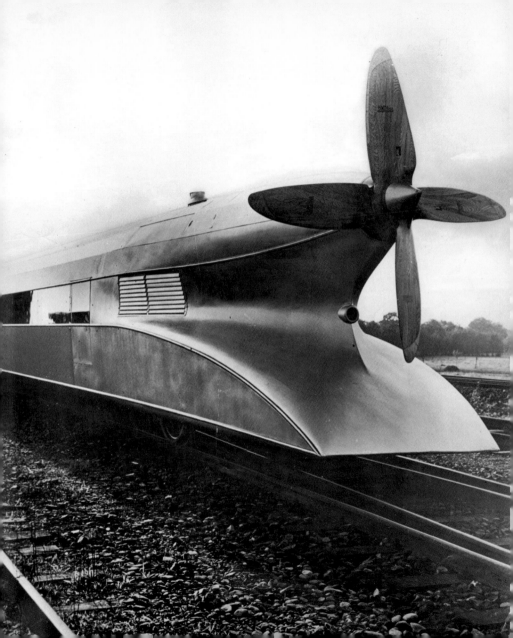

9. Transport
Verkehrswesen
Moyens de transport

Faster… John Cobb broke the land speed record at Bonneville Salt Flats in 1938 and 1939. His car reached over 369 mph (590 kph). The steam locomotive *Mallard* pulled a seven-coach train weighing 240 tonnes at 126 mph (202 kph) on 3 July 1938. The following month the *Queen Mary* regained the Blue Riband by crossing the Atlantic in the record time of 3 days and 21 hours.

Further… It was possible to board the *Twentieth Century Limited* in New York – with many movie and radio stars for company – and travel to California with just one change. The *Orient Express* steamed its way from France to Istanbul. Trains sweated their way across the 496-mile (794-kilometre) Nullarbor Plain in Australia. In the skies, new air routes opened across the world, following the trails blazed by solo pioneers like Amy Johnson, Amelia Earhart and Sir Charles Kingsford Smith.

Safer… The days of deadly icebergs were over, the nights of submarine menace yet to come. The rich floated safely over the oceans of the world in the luxury of palatial liners. The newly imposed speed limits and traffic lights lessened the appalling loss of life on roads.

But the *Hindenburg* and R 101 disasters brought the age of the airship to a premature end.

Schneller… John Cobb brach mit seinem Wagen 1938 und 1939 auf der Salztonebene von Bonneville den Geschwindigkeitsweltrekord mit über 590 km/h. Die Dampflokomotive *Mallard* zog am 3. Juli 1938 sieben Waggons mit einem Gesamtgewicht von 240 Tonnen und erreichte dabei 202 km/h. Einen Monat später überquerte die *Queen Mary* den Atlantik in der Bestzeit von 3 Tagen und 21 Stunden und eroberte damit das Blaue Band zurück.

Weiter… Man konnte an Bord der *Twentieth Century Limited* von New York nach Kalifornien reisen, dabei die Gesellschaft zahlreicher Film- und Radio-Stars genießen und mußte auf der langen Fahrt sogar nur einmal umsteigen. Der *Orientexpreß* schnaufte von

Frankreich nach Istanbul, während andere Eisenbahnen auf einer Strecke von 794 Kilometern die australische Nullarbor-Ebene durchquerten. Am Himmel eröffneten sich neue Flugrouten, die die ganze Welt umspannten und von Pionieren der Luftfahrt wie Amy Johnson, Amelia Earhart und Sir Charles Kingsford Smith erkundet worden waren.

Sicherer … Die Tage der todbringenden Eisberge waren vorüber, aber die Bedrohung durch feindliche U-Boote stand noch bevor. Die Reichen glitten ungefährdet über die Weltmeere, umgeben vom Luxus der palastähnlichen Liniendampfer. Neu erlassene Geschwindigkeitsbeschränkungen und Ampeln sorgten dafür, daß weit weniger Menschen im Straßenverkehr ums Leben kamen als zuvor.

Einzig die Katastrophen der *Hindenburg* und der R 101 beendeten vorzeitig das große Zeitalter der Luftschiffe.

Toujours plus vite… John Cobb battit le record du monde de vitesse à Bonneville Salt Flats en 1938 et en 1939. Sa voiture dépassa les 590 km/heure. Le 3 juillet 1938, la locomotive à vapeur *Mallard* tira un train de sept wagons pesant 240 tonnes à la vitesse de 202 km/heure. En août, le *Queen Mary* traversait l'Atlantique en un temps record de 3 jours et 21 heures et décrocha à nouveau le Ruban bleu.

Toujours plus loin… A New York, il était possible de monter dans la *Twentieth Century Limited* – en compagnie de nombreuses vedettes du cinéma et de la radio – et de gagner la Californie en effectuant un seul changement. L'*Orient Express* reliait à toute vapeur la France à Istanbul. En Australie, les trains parcouraient 794 kilomètres à travers la plaine aride de Nullarbor. Dans le ciel, de nouvelles routes se dessinaient d'un bout à l'autre du monde sur les traces des pionniers solitaires tels que Amy Johnson, Amelia Earhart et Sir Charles Kingsford Smith.

Toujours plus sûr… L'époque des icebergs meurtriers était révolue, celle des sous-marins s'annonçant . Les riches traversaient les océans du monde entier en toute sécurité, à bord de luxueux palaces flottants. Les limites de vitesse, nouvellement imposées, et les feux rouges réduisirent le nombre de morts sur les routes, effroyable jusque-là.

Mais la catastrophe du zeppelin *Hindenburg* et celle du R 101 mirent un terme prématuré à l'ère du dirigeable.

World ambassador for luxury flight. A group of
Berlin *Schupos* (policemen) help to land and anchor
the *Graf Zeppelin*, 1935. Of all the giant airships,
the *Graf Zeppelin* had the finest safety record.

Der weltweite Botschafter für Luxusflugreisen.
Eine Gruppe Berliner Schupos (Schutzpolizisten)
hilft mit, den gigantischen *Graf Zeppelin* zu landen
und zu verankern, 1935. Was die Sicherheit anbetraf,
genoß dieses Luftschiff den allerbesten Ruf.

Ambassadeur du vol de luxe dans le monde
entier. Un comité de la police de Berlin aide le
Graf Zeppelin à se poser au sol, 1935. De tous
les dirigeables géants, le *Graf Zeppelin* était sans
conteste le plus sûr.

Huge crowds gather
in Tokyo to admire
the *Graf Zeppelin*,
1930. At the
beginning of the
Thirties, airships
dominated
international air
travel, though
doubts had been
expressed about
safety even in the
Twenties.

Enorme Menschen-
mengen versammeln
sich 1930 in Tokio,
um den *Graf Zeppe-
lin* zu bewundern.
Zu Beginn der drei-
ßiger Jahre domi-
nierten Luftschiffe
den internationalen
Flugverkehr, obwohl
bereits in den zwan-
ziger Jahren Zweifel
an deren Sicherheit
angemeldet worden
waren.

Une foule
gigantesque s'est
réunie pour admirer
le *Graf Zeppelin* à
Tokyo, 1930. Au
début des années
trente, les dirigeables
représentaient le
premier moyen de
transport aérien
international même
si, dès les années
vingt, des réserves
avaient été
exprimées quant à
leur sécurité.

May 1938. John
Cobb in his Railton
Racer at Brooklands
Race Track, England.
It was the year he
first broke the world
land speed record.

Mai 1938. John
Cobb in seinem
Railton-Rennwagen
auf der Rennstrecke
Brooklands,
England. In jenem
Jahr brach er zum
ersten Mal den
Geschwindigkeits-
weltrekord.

Mai 1938. John
Cobb dans son engin
de course fabriqué
par Railton sur le
circuit de
Brooklands,
Angleterre. Cette
année-là, il battit
pour la première fois
le record du monde
de vitesse
automobile.

George Eyton's
streamlined car
behind guarded
doors at
Wolverhampton,
England, August
1937.

George Eytons
stromlinienförmi-
ges Autohinter
verschlossenen
Türen im
britischen
Wolverhampton,
August 1937.

La voiture à
vapeur de George
Eyton dans un
bâtiment placé
sous surveillance à
Wolverhampton,
Angleterre, août
1937.

Working on the Bennie Railplane, 1930. This was an experimental passenger train to
be driven by air turbines. It was planned to run on a monorail suspended from girders,
but, like many Thirties innovations, it was not commercially viable.

Der Bau des Bennie-Schienenflugzeugs, 1930. Dieses Versuchsmodell eines
Personenverkehrszugs trieben Druckluftturbinen an. Ursprünglich sollte es als
Einschienenbahn auf einer Laufschiene mit Trägeraufhängung eingesetzt werden. Doch
dieser Plan war, wie so viele Innovationen der dreißiger Jahre, finanziell unrentabel.

A l'œuvre sur le train-avion de Bennie, 1930. C'était un train de voyageurs
expérimental conçu avec des turbines à air. Il aurait dû circuler sur un monorail
suspendu à des poutrelles mais, à l'instar de nombreuses inventions des années trente,
le projet ne fut pas viable commercialement.

1931. Flight Lieutenant F W Long is carried ashore from S1595, a Vickers Supermarine S6B. The plane won the 12th annual Schneider Trophy Race at a speed of 341 mph (546 kph).

1931. Oberleutnant der Luftwaffe F. W. Long wird von der S1595, einer Vickers Supermarine S6B, an Land getragen. Das Flugzeug gewann das 12. alljährliche Rennen der Schneider Trophy mit einer Geschwindigkeit von 546 km/h.

1931. Le lieutenant F. W. Long est ramené à terre à sa descente d'avion, un S1595-Vickers Supermarine S6B qui remporta, à 546 km/heure, le Trophée Schneider lors du 12e Championnat annuel de vitesse.

One of the four
giant Turbiston
bronze propellers
for the German
transatlantic liner
Europa at the
manufacturers in
London, 1936.

Eine der vier
bronzenen Schiffs-
schrauben, die für
den deutschen Trans-
atlantikdampfer
Europa bestimmt
waren, beim
Londoner Hersteller
Turbiston, 1936.

Une des quatre
hélices géantes en
bronze fabriquées
pour le trans-
atlantique allemand
Europa par les usines
Turbiston à Londres,
1936.

1933. The *Prinz-regent Luitpold* passes under the Forth Bridge, keel uppermost. The ship was part of the German fleet · scuttled at Scapa Flow in 1919.

1933. Die *Prinz-regent Luitpold* passiert die Forth Bridge mit dem Kiel nach oben. Das Schiff war Teil der deutschen Flotte, die 1919 bei Scapa Flow versenkt worden war.

1933. Le *Prinzregent Luitpold* passe sous le pont de Forth, la quille bien au-dessus du niveau de l'eau. Ce bâtiment faisait partie de la flotte allemande sabordée à Scapa en 1919.

Ivan Shagin's
photograph of
Soviet citizens
celebrating the 1936
Aviation Day in
Tushino, Moscow.

Auf dieser Aufnahme
Iwan Schagins feiern
1936 sowjetische
Bürger in Moskau
den Tag der
Luftfahrt.

Citoyens soviétiques
célébrant la Journée
de l'Aviation à
Tushino, Moscou,
en 1936 et
photographiés par
Ivan Shagin.

A view from the rear gunner's seat in a 99B Squadron bomber at an air pageant, Northolt Aerodrome, London, June 1933. At the time, both biplanes probably constituted the cream of Royal Air Force machines.

Die Aussicht des hinteren Bordschützen in einem 99B-Staffelbomber bei einer Flugschau im Londoner Northolt Aerodrome, Juni 1933. Zu jener Zeit gehörten die beiden Doppeldecker wohl zu den besten Maschinen der Royal Air Force.

Vue à partir du siège arrière du canonier d'un bombardier d'escadrille 99B lors d'une fête de l'air à l'aérodrome de Northolt, Londres, juin 1933. A l'époque, ces deux biplans constituaient probablement les meilleurs avions de la Royal Air Force.

October 1933.
The New York
Midnight Follies
arrive at Croydon
Airport, London.
The plane is
Horatius, one of
the Handley Page
Hannibal Class
in use by Imperial
Airways.

Oktober 1933. Die
New Yorker
Midnight Follies bei
ihrer Ankunft auf
dem Londoner
Flughafen Croydon.
Das Flugzeug hieß
Horatius und war
eine Maschine von
Handley Pages
Hannibal-Klasse, die
von Imperial
Airways eingesetzt
wurde.

Octobre 1933. La
troupe du New York
Midnight Follies à
son arrivée à
l'aéroport de
Croydon, Londres.
L'avion, surnommé
Horatius, faisait
partie de la flotte des
Handley Page
Hannibal utilisés par
Imperial Airways.

August 1934. Holidaymakers on Jersey in the Channel islands pose for the camera before setting off on a joyride. Many pilots from World War I eked out a living offering 'ten minute hops' from grass runways at seaside resorts.

August 1934. Urlauber auf der Kanalinsel Jersey posieren vor der Kamera, bevor sie zu einem Vergnügungsflug starten. Viele ehemalige Flieger des Ersten Weltkrieges schlugen sich mehr schlecht als recht durch, indem sie in Seebädern „Zehn-Minuten-Flüge" anboten und Grasflächen als Start- und Landebahnen nutzten.

Août 1934. Des vacancières à Jersey, une île de la Manche, posent avant de décoller. Beaucoup de pilotes de la Première Guerre mondiale arrondissaient leurs fins de mois sur les pistes des stations balnéaires en proposant des « vols de dix minutes ».

June 1937.
The streamlined
Coronation Scot on
a test run to Crewe.
The train had been
named to celebrate
the coronation of
George VI in May.

Juni 1937. Der
stromlinienförmige
Coronation Scot auf
eine Probefahrt nach
Crewe. Der Zug
erhielt seinen
Namen zur Feier der
Krönung Georgs VI.
im Mai des Jahres.

Juin 1937. La
Coronation Scot
effectue un essai sur
le trajet de Crewe.
Ce train à vapeur
avait été ainsi baptisé
pour commémorer
le couronnement de
Georges VI en mai.

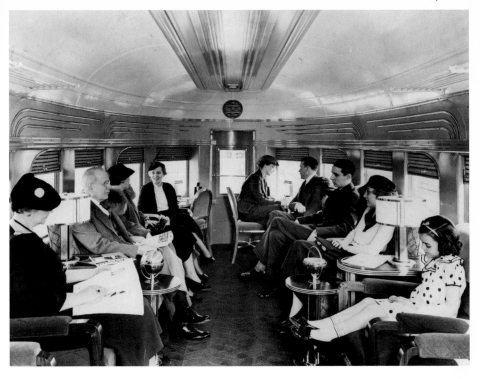

The streamlined lounge and observation car of the diesel-powered *Green Diamond* of the Illinois Central railroad system. The new train had been introduced to speed services to Chicago.

Der stromlinienförmige Salon- und Panoramawagen des *Green Diamond* der Illinois Central Eisenbahngesellschaft. Dieser neue Zug mit Diesellok ermöglichte eine schnellere Verbindung nach Chicago.

Salon de repos et d'observation du *Green Diamond*, un train diesel de la compagnie de l'Illinois Central. Il avait été mis en circulation pour accélérer le service à destination de Chicago.

The Standard Motor Company's convention luncheon at the shop floor in
Coventry, March 1936. The luncheon included a parade of new models.
Standard Motor's successes in the Thirties were the 'Big Nine' and 'Big
Sixteen', the first cars with an integrated fire-extinguishing system.

Bei einem Tagungsessen der Standard Motor Company in Coventry im März
1936 werden die neuen Automodelle vorgeführt. Standard Motors größte
Erfolge in den dreißiger Jahren waren der „Big Nine" und der „Big Sixteen",
die ersten Wagen mit integrierter Feuerlöschanlage.

Déjeuner dans un atelier de la Standard Motor Company à Coventry, mars
1936, et présentation des nouveaux modèles. Les deux grands succès de
Stantard Motor dans les années trente furent la « Big Nine » et la « Big
Sixteen », les premières voitures disposant d'un système de démarrage intégré.

June 1938. Coaches from the Channel Islands Boat Express are hauled through the streets of Weymouth by a humble tank engine. A flagman sits on the front of the locomotive, ringing a bell to warn pedestrians of the train's approach.

Juni 1938. Eine bescheidene Dampflok zieht Waggons des Schiffsexpresses der Kanalinseln durch die Straßen von Weymouth. Mit einer Glocke warnt ein auf der Lokomotive sitzender Eisenbahner Fußgänger vor dem herannahenden Zug.

Juin 1938. Des wagons de la compagnie Channel Islands Boat Express sont remorqués à travers les rues de Weymouth par une simple locomotive à tender. Assis à l'avant du train, un employé agite une cloche pour avertir les piétons du passage du train.

In the age when everything had to be streamlined – a streamlined truck body rests on a standard 2-ton Commer chassis at Wembley, December 1933. Streamlining was expensive, and the added aerodynamic body parts made maintenance more difficult.

Im Zeitalter der Aerodynamik. Eine stromlinienförmige Karosserie ruht auf dem Standardchassis eines Commer Zweitonners in Wembley, Dezember 1933. Die Herstellung von aerodynamischen Fahrzeugen war kostspielig, und die zusätzlichen Karosserieteile erschwerten obendrein ihre Wartung.

A cette époque, tout devait être aérodynamique. La carrosserie de ce camion aérodynamique est posée sur un châssis Commer standard de deux tonnes, Wembley, décembre 1933. La rationalisation était coûteuse, les pièces de carrosserie aérodynamiques rendant l'entretien plus difficile encore.

1935. An aerial view
of a traffic jam at
the entrance to the
Holland Tunnel in
New York.

1935. Ein Verkehrs-
stau an der Einfahrt
zum New Yorker
Holland Tunnel.

1935. Vue aérienne
d'un embouteillage
à l'entrée du tunnel
Holland à New
York.

London, 1939. Two attempts to beat petrol rationing following the outbreak of war. A woman drives a car said to be capable of covering 80 miles (130 kilometres) to a gallon of petrol. If she ran out of petrol she could always tuck the car under her arm and walk home with it.

London 1939. Zwei Versuche, der zu Kriegsbeginn verhängten Benzinrationierung ein Schnippchen zu schlagen. Der Wagen dieser Dame verbrauchte Berichten zufolge auf 130 Kilometern nur 4,5 Liter Benzin. Falls ihr das Benzin ausging, konnte sie den Wagen unter dem Arm nach Hause tragen.

Londres, 1939. Deux manières de faire face au rationnement de l'essence instauré au début de la guerre. Cette femme conduit une voiture censée parcourir 130 kilomètres avec seulement 4,5 litres d'essence. Si elle tombait en panne d'essence, il lui suffirait de prendre la voiture sous son bras et de rentrer à pied.

November 1939. A tiny Velocar moves slowly through
Hyde Park, London. The car was powered by two
pedals, like a child's toy. It was probably quicker to walk.

November 1939. Ein Tretauto bewegt sich gemächlich
durch den Londoner Hyde Park. Der Wagen wurde wie
ein Kinderfahrzeug mit zwei Pedalen angetrieben.
Zu Fuß hätte man sein Ziel wohl schneller erreicht.

Londres, novembre 1939. Une mini vélo-voiture
traversant Hyde Park à faible allure. Le véhicule était
actionné par deux pédales, comme un jouet. Circuler
à pied était sans doute plus rapide.

February 1936. Miss Victoria Worsley, a driving instructor,
teaches one of her pupils how to reverse round a corner.
Driving tests had been introduced two years earlier.

Februar 1936. Die Fahrlehrerin Miss Victoria Worsley
zeigt einem Schüler, wie man rückwärts um eine Kurve
fährt. Zwei Jahre zuvor war die Führerscheinprüfung
eingeführt worden.

Février 1936. Mlle Victoria Worsley, monitrice d'auto-
école, apprend à un élève comment faire marche arrière
au coin d'une rue. Le permis de conduire était obligatoire
depuis deux ans.

February 1937.
The new 30mph
sign, Westway,
London. For a
disastrous few years,
Britain scrapped
the speed limit on
roads altogether.

Februar 1937. Ein
neues Verkehrsschild
am Londoner
Westway, das die
Geschwindigkeit von
über 30 Meilen pro
Stunde untersagt.
Für einige, tragische
Jahre wurden die
Geschwindigkeits-
beschränkungen auf
britischen Straßen
aufgehoben.

Février 1937. Le
nouveau panneau de
signalisation limitant
la vitesse à 30 miles
à l'heure, Westway,
Londres. Pendant
quelques années, qui
furent désastreuses,
la Grande-Bretagne
abandonna toute
idée de limiter la
vitesse sur les routes.

10. Sport
Sport
Le Sport

Jesse Owens at the start of the 200 metres final in Berlin, 1936.
Owens won in the Olympic record time of 20.7 seconds. He won
four gold medals altogether. Lutz Long, the German athlete who
came second to Owens in the Long Jump, became a close friend.

Jesse Owens beim Endlauf über 200 Meter in Berlin, 1936. Er
siegte mit der neuen olympischen Rekordzeit von 20,7 Sekunden
und gewann insgesamt vier Goldmedaillen. Der deutsche Athlet
Lutz Long, der hinter Owens den zweiten Platz im Weitsprung
belegte, wurde einer seiner besten Freunde.

Jesse Owens au départ de la finale du 200 mètres à Berlin, 1936.
Owens gagna la course en 20,7 secondes, battant ainsi le record
olympique. Il obtint en tout quatre médailles d'or. Lutz Long,
l'athlète allemand qui fut second après Owens au saut en
longueur, devint son grand ami.

10. Sport
Sport
Le Sport

It was a time of high drama in sport. 'Bodyline' bowling in a cricket tour of Australia threatened to rupture Anglo-Australian relations. The triumphalism of the 1936 Berlin Olympic Games, filmed by Leni Riefenstahl, was destroyed by the black athlete Jesse Owens.

International football came of age with the first World Cup competition, organized in South America and virtually ignored by Europe save for those countries that sent teams – France, Romania and Belgium. A crowd of 100,000 saw Uruguay beat Argentina 4-3.

Like most aspects of life in the Thirties, it was a sporting age of the masses. Huge crowds gathered to watch football, rugby, skating, marathon dance competitions and any type of racing – horse, greyhound, car, motorcycle and aeroplane.

Records were created and then shattered on an almost daily basis. Australia's Don Bradman emerged as the most efficient cricket machine of all time. Fred Perry gave British tennis its last Wimbledon glory for a couple of generations. Mussolini had better luck than Hitler, when he saw Italy beat Czechoslovakia in the second World Cup final in 1934.

And in 1932 a film camera proved that a goal should have been disallowed in a Wembley Cup Final – shades of things to come.

In sportlicher Hinsicht waren die dreißiger Jahre ein hochdramatisches Jahrzehnt. Ein unvorhergesehener Zwischenfall während einer Kricket-Tournee durch Australien trübten allerdings die anglo-australischen Beziehungen. Der Triumph der Olympischen Spiele 1936 in Berlin, gefilmt von Leni Riefenstahl, wurde von dem schwarzen Athleten Jesse Owens niedergeschlagen.

Der Fußballsport hatte an Status gewonnen. Die erste Fußballweltmeisterschaft fand in Südamerika statt und stieß in Europa kaum auf Interesse – außer bei den Teilnehmerländern

Frankreich, Rumänien und Belgien. 100.000 Zuschauer sahen das Endspiel, in dem Uruguay Argentinien mit 4:3 schlug.

Wie in den meisten Lebensbereichen der dreißiger Jahre spielten auch im Sport die Massen eine entscheidende Rolle. Menschenmengen verfolgten live Fußball, Rugby, Eiskunstlauf, Wettbewerbe im Marathontanzen oder verschiedene Arten von Rennen: Pferderennen, Windhundrennen, Autorennen, Motorradrennen oder Wettflüge.

Fast täglich wurden neue Rekorde aufgestellt und wieder gebrochen. Der Australier Don Bradman wurde der beste Kricketspieler aller Zeiten. Fred Perry schenkte dem britischen Tennis seinen letzten Wimbledonsieg für mehrere Generationen. Und Mussolini hatte mehr Glück als Hitler, als er bei der zweiten Fußballweltmeisterschaft 1934 dabei war, als Italien die Tschechoslowakei besiegte.

Und 1932 bewies schließlich in einem Endspiel in Wembley eine Filmkamera, daß ein Tor nicht hätte gegeben werden dürfen – ein richtungsweisendes Ereignis für die Sportwelt.

Ce fut une époque riche en drames pour le sport. Un incident survenu au cours d'un grand tournoi de cricket menaça de rompre les relations anglo-australiennes. Le triomphalisme des Jeux olympiques de Berlin en 1936, filmé par Leni Riefenstahl, fut anéanti par l'athlète noir Jesse Owens.

Le football devint international. La première Coupe du monde fut organisée en Amérique du Sud mais dédaignée par l'Europe, à l'exception de la France, de la Roumanie et de la Belgique. 100 000 personnes assistèrent au match qui vit l'Uruguay battre l'Argentine par 4 buts à 3.

Le sport, dans les années trente, suscita l'enthousiasme des masses. Des foules énormes assistaient à des matchs de football, de rugby, à des concours de patins à glace, à des marathons de danse et à des courses de toutes sortes : chevaux, lévriers, voitures, motos et avions.

Presque chaque jour, des records établis étaient aussitôt battus. L'Australien Don Bradman devint le meilleur joueur de cricket de tous les temps. Le tennis britannique, grâce à Fred Perry, connut la gloire à Wimbledon, la dernière avant longtemps. En 1934, Mussolini assista à la victoire de l'Italie contre la Tchécoslovaquie en finale de la deuxième Coupe du monde.

Enfin, en 1932, un film démontra qu'un but marqué en finale de la Coupe de Wembley aurait dû être annulé – c'était l'aube d'une nouvelle époque.

Jesse Owens is off to a flyer. His three other gold medals were in the 100 metres and the 4x100 metres relay and the long jump. When he won the 200 metres, the whole stadium rose in tribute to the black athlete from Ohio State. Hitler had already left.

Jesse Owens startet zum Sieg. Er hatte bereits drei Goldmedaillen gewonnen, über 100 Meter, der 4x100-Meter-Staffel und im Weitsprung. Als er im Lauf über 200 Meter siegte, erhoben sich alle Zuschauer als Zeichen der Anerkennung für den schwarzen Athleten aus Ohio – Hitler hatte zu diesem Zeitpunkt das Stadion bereits verlassen.

Jesse Owens décolle vers la victoire. Il avait déjà gagné trois médailles d'or, une pour le 100 mètres, une pour le relais du 4x100 mètres et une en saut en langueur . Lorsqu'il gagna le 200 mètres, tout le stade se leva pour ovationner l'athlète noir de l'Ohio. Hitler avait déjà quitté les lieux.

Käthe Krauß in tears
after a bad handover
cost the German
women's team gold
in the 4x100 metres
relay, August 1936.
It wasn't her fault.

Käthe Krauß weint
nach einer miß-
glückten Übergabe,
die das deutsche
Team in der 4x100-
Meter-Staffel die
Goldmedaille
kostete, August
1936. Sie traf dabei
keine Schuld.

Käthe Krauß en
pleurs après un
mauvais passage du
témoin qui coûta la
médaille d'or aux
Allemandes dans le
relais du 4x100
mètres, août 1936.
Ce n'était pourtant
pas sa faute.

The start of a motorcycle race during the Berlin Olympics,
1936. Motorcycling was not part of the Olympics, but
the sport was enormously popular and glamorous during
the Thirties.

Am Start eines Motorradrennens während der Olympischen
Spiele in Berlin, 1936. Motorradfahren war zwar keine
olympische Disziplin, es war jedoch in den dreißiger Jahren
ein ungeheuer beliebter und bewunderter Sport.

Départ d'une course de motos aux Jeux olympiques de Berlin,
1936. La moto ne faisait pas partie des épreuves olympiques
mais ce sport était très populaire dans les années trente.

A phalanx of officials at the Berlin Olympics. Timings lacked the
accuracy of modern athletics. Each official timed a different runner, but
whether all stop watches started simultaneously is debatable.

Sportfunktionäre bei den Olympischen Spielen in Berlin. Die Zeiten
wurden damals nicht mit der heute üblichen Genauigkeit gemessen. Jeder
dieser Herren nahm die Zeit eines bestimmten Läufers, man konnte
allerdings nicht prüfen, ob alle Stoppuhren gleichzeitig gestartet wurden.

Brochette d'officiels aux Jeux olympiques de Berlin. Le chronométrage
n'était pas aussi précis qu'aujourd'hui. Chaque officiel chronométrait un
athlète différent – reste à savoir s'ils appuyaient tous en même temps sur
leur montre.

August 1933. Just a few months after Hitler is appointed chancellor, a team of German athletes give the Nazi salute while their national anthem is played at the White City, London. Five years later, an English football team gave the same salute in Berlin.

August 1933. Wenige Monate nach Hitlers Ernennung zum Reichskanzler, entbieten deutsche Athleten zur Nationalhymne den Hitlergruß im Londoner Stadion White City. Fünf Jahre später begrüßte eine englische Fußballmannschaft mit derselben Geste die Zuschauer in Berlin.

Août 1933. Quelques mois après la nomination de Hitler au poste de chancelier, des athlètes allemands font le salut nazi pendant leur hymne national au stade White City, Londres. Cinq ans plus tard, une équipe de football anglaise fit le même salut à Berlin.

Ball markers in the
Gleneagles gloom,
Scotland, 1936.
The occasion was
the Ryder Cup golf
match between
Britain and the
United States.

Ballmarkierer in der
düsteren Landschaft
der schottischen
Gleneagles, 1936.
Sie unterstützten die
Golfspieler im
Wettkampf zwischen
Großbritannien und
den USA um den
Ryder Cup.

Temps de chien pour
les marqueurs de
balles à Gleneagles
en Ecosse, 1936.
Partie de golf
opposant les Etats-
Unis à la Grande-
Bretagne lors de la
Ryder Cup.

The Arsenal football team gather round a mobile television unit, 1937. They were the first English footballers to be seen on television, in a practice game against Arsenal Reserves. The 1938 Cup Final – between Preston and Huddersfield – was the first to be televised, to an audience of 10,000.

Die Mannschaft des Fußballvereins Arsenal schart sich um eine Filmkamera, 1937. Sie waren die ersten englischen Fußballer, die man im Fernsehen bewundern konnte, und zwar in einem Trainingsspiel gegen Ersatzspieler desselben Clubs. Das Pokalendspiel von 1938 – zwischen Preston und Huddersfield – war das erste Endspiel, das übertragen wurde, und es erreichte 10.000 Menschen über den Bildschirm.

Joueurs de l'équipe d'Arsenal autour d'une caméra de télévision, 1937. Ils furent les premiers footballeurs anglais à apparaître à la télévision lors d'un match d'entraînement. La finale de la Coupe de 1938, entre Preston et Huddersfield, fut retransmise pour la première fois devant 10 000 spectateurs.

The English captain
Blenkinsop shakes
hands with his
Spanish opposite
number, Ricardo
Zamora, Highbury,
1931. England
won 7-1.

Der Kapitän der
englischen National-
mannschaft,
Blenkinsop, begrüßt
in Highbury den
Spielführer der
spanischen Mann-
schaft, Ricardo
Zamora, 1931.
England gewann mit
7:1 Toren.

Le capitaine anglais
Blenkinsop serre la
main de son
homologue
espagnol, Ricardo
Zamora, Highbury,
1931. L'Angleterre
gagna 7 à 1.

The Wembley crowd, April 1932. Newcastle beat Arsenal 2-1 in the Cup
Final, but Movietone News cameras showed after the game that their first
goal should have been disallowed. That night the referee, Mr W Harper,
insisted, 'It was a goal... as God is my judge!'

Zuschauer im Wembley-Stadion, April 1932. Newcastle schlug Arsenal in
diesem Pokalfinale mit 2:1 Toren. Kamera-Aufzeichnungen der Movietone
News zeigten jedoch nach Spielende, daß das erste Tor der Mannschaft aus
Newcastle eigentlich nicht hätte gegeben werden dürfen. Schiedsrichter W.
Harper insistierte damals: „Es war ein Tor ... und Gott ist mein Zeuge!"

La foule de Wembley, avril 1932. Newcastle battit Arsenal 2 à 1 en finale de
la Coupe mais les caméras de Movietone News montrèrent après le match que
le premier but de Newcastle aurait dû être annulé. Le même soir, l'arbitre,
W. Harper, déclara que » le but avait été marqué et que Dieu était son juge ! «

March 1933. West Ham supporters in ebullient
mood for the FA Cup Semi-Final against Everton.
The match was played at Wolverhampton. Everton
won 2-1, and went on to win the Final.

März 1933. Fußballfans von West Ham beim
Halbfinalspiel gegen Everton um den Fußballpokal.
Die Begegnung, die in Wolverhampton stattfand,
gewann Everton mit 2:1 Toren, und dieser Verein
siegte schließlich auch im Endspiel.

Mars 1933. Des supporters de West Ham en
grande forme lors de la demi-finale de la Coupe de
la FA jouée à Wolverhampton contre Everton qui
gagna 2 à 1 et qui allait remporter la finale.

June 1930. A women's tug-of-war team in the Lyons Club annual sports at Sudbury, near London. Lyons owned a vast string of hotels, restaurants and tea shops, and employed thousands of women as 'nippies' (waitresses), serving 160 million meals a day.

Juni 1930. Eine Frauenmannschaft beim Tauziehen während des alljährlichen Sportfests des Lyons Clubs in Sudbury bei London. Zur Lyons-Kette gehörten Hotels, Restaurants und Teestuben, in denen Tausende von Kellnerinnen arbeiteten und täglich 160 Millionen Mahlzeiten servierten.

Juin 1930. Equipe féminine de tir à la corde lors du tournoi annuel du Lyons Club à Sudbury, près de Londres. Lyons possédait un grand réseau d'hôtels, de restaurants et de salons de thé, employant des milliers de serveuses et distribuant plus de 160 millions de repas par jour.

A lone goalkeeper
practises in an empty
football stadium,
1939. Football was
to take a back seat
for five years.

Ein einsamer
Torhüter trainiert in
einem leeren
Stadion, 1939. Der
Fußballsport mußte
in den folgenden
fünf Jahren hinter
Wichtigerem
zurückstehen.

Un gardien de but
s'entraîne seul au
milieu d'un stade
vide, 1939. Le
football allait être
mis au rancart
les cinq années
suivantes.

April 1938.
Don Bradman, the
Australian batsman,
gets a telegram on
the pitch at
Worcester. He was
in the middle of
scoring 258.

April 1938.
Dem australischen
Schlagmann Don
Bradman wird auf
dem Spielfeld in
Worcester ein Tele-
gramm zugestellt, als
er gerade im Begriff
ist, ein Punkte-
ergebnis von 258 zu
erzielen.

Avril 1938. Remise
d'un télégramme à
Don Bradman, le
batteur australien,
sur le terrain de
Worcester. Il était
sur le point de
marquer 258 points.

Brisbane, March 1933. Australian batsman Woodfull ducks to avoid a
ball from Larwood in the 'Bodyline' tour. Later, Woodfull was hit just
above the heart. In the Australian dressing room, the England manager
was met with the words, 'There's two teams out there and only one
of them's playing cricket.'

Brisbane, März 1933. Der australische Schlagmann Woodfull duckt
sich, um einem Wurf auszuweichen, den Larwood ausführte. Kurze
Zeit später wurde Woodfull knapp über dem Herzen getroffen. Als der
Trainer der englischen Mannschaft die Umkleideräume der Australier
betrat, begrüßte man ihn mit den Worten: „Da draußen befinden sich
zwei Mannschaften, von denen aber nur eine Kricket spielt."

Brisbane, mars 1933. L'Australien Woodfull évite la balle de Larwood
durant le tournoi de la Bodyline. Plus tard, il fut touché près du coeur.
Dans les vestiaires australiens, le manager anglais fut accueilli par ces
mots « Il y a deux équipes là dehors mais une seule joue au cricket. »

The tea break during
the Leeds Test,
England v Australia,
1938. Bradman
failed for once,
making only 103.

Eine Teepause
während des
Testmatches England
gegen Australien in
Leeds, 1938.
Bradman hatte hier
ausnahmsweise einen
schlechten Tag und
erzielte nur 103
Punkte.

Pause pour le thé
durant le Tournoi de
Leeds opposant
l'Angleterre à
l'Australie, 1938.
Bradman échoua
pour une fois,
marquant seulement
103 points.

July 1931. The Surrey and England cricketer, Andy Sandham, coaching children at the Foundling Hospital, London. Sandham scored over a hundred centuries in first class cricket, and was the first batsman to score a triple century in a Test match.

Juli 1931. Andy Sandham, der Kricket für Surrey spielte und auch der National-mannschaft angehörte, trainiert mit Kindern des Foundling Hospitals in London. Sandham war ein Spitzenspieler, der als erster Schlagmann eine dreifache Hundert in einem Testmatch erzielte.

Juillet 1931. Le joueur de cricket de Surrey et de l'équipe d'Angleterre, Andy Sandham, avec des enfants à l'Hôpital de Foundling, Londres. Il marqua des centaines de points en matchs de première ligue et fut le premier à faire un triple cent points dans un match international.

Children snatch a glimpse of cricket at The Oval, London, 1933. The fence round
the ground was at that time full of gaps and cracks. Many children successfully
sneaked in without paying. Today there is an impenetrable brick wall.

Kricketbegeisterte Kinder erhaschen einen Blick auf das Londoner Spielfeld
The Oval, 1933. Damals hatte der Lattenzaun, der das Gelände umgab, eine
Menge Ritzen und Spalten, und vielen Kindern gelang es, sich ohne Eintrittskarte
unter die Zuschauer zu mischen. Heute umgibt die Anlage eine unüberwindbare
Steinmauer.

Match de cricket suivi par des enfants depuis l'extérieur de l'Oval, Londres, 1933.
A cette époque, beaucoup d'enfants réussissaient à entrer sans payer, la barrière
étant pleine de brèches. Aujourd'hui, il y a un mur de briques infranchissable.

March 1937. A game of 'squashette' at the Dulwich Municipal
Baths, London. The player on the right is Fred Dyer who
invented this portable squash court. It was not a success.

März 1937. Zwei Herren spielen „Squashette" im Stadtbad
des Londoner Stadtteils Dulwich. Der Spieler zur Rechten, der
diesen tragbaren Squashcourt entwarf, ist Fred Dyer. Es gelang
ihm nicht, seine Erfindung erfolgreich zu vermarkten.

Mars 1937. Partie de « mini-squash » aux Bains municipaux
de Dulwich, Londres. Le joueur de droite est Fred Dyer,
l'inventeur de ce court de squash portatif.

A member of the
Oxford crew
practises in front of
a mirror for the
1935 University
Boat Race. Oxford
lost for the 12th
time in succession.

Ein Ruderer der
Mannschaft aus
Oxford übt seine
Bewegungen vor
dem Spiegel, im
Hinblick auf die
Regatta der
Universitäten 1935.
Oxford verlor in
jenem Jahr bereits
zum zwölften Mal
hintereinander.

Un membre de
l'équipe d'Oxford
s'entraîne devant un
miroir en vue de la
Course d'aviron des
universités de 1935.
Oxford perdit pour
la 12e fois
consécutive.

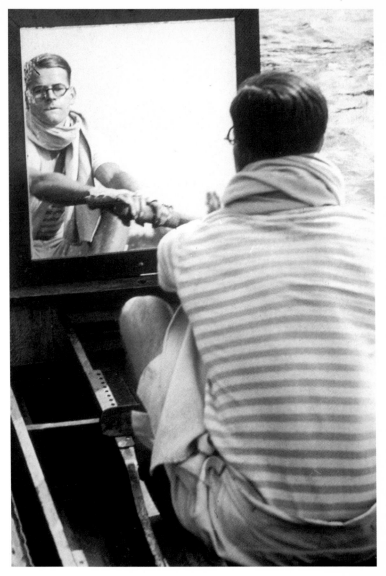

March 1932. A cross-country race between cyclists and
harriers at Enfield, near London. Novelty competitions
such as this were frequent and popular in the Thirties.

März 1932. Ein Querfeldeinrennen zwischen
Radfahrern und Geländeläufern bei Enfield in der
Nähe von London. In den dreißiger Jahren waren
solche ungewöhnlichen Wettbewerbe sehr beliebt.

Mars 1932. Course à travers champs opposant cyclistes
et coureurs de cross à Enfield, près de Londres. Dans les
années trente, les nouveautés en matière de compétitions
sportives étaient courantes et fort populaires.

June 1938. At a motorcycle rodeo in the grounds of the Crystal Palace, London. The riders are practising a surfboarding technique. The park was the venue for many sports: sidecar polo, midget-car racing, boxing, speedway, cricket and even dog and cat shows.

Juni 1938. Ein Motorrad-Rodeo auf dem Gelände des Londoner Kristallpalastes. Die Fahrer trainieren die Surfboard-Technik. In diesem Park wurden auch zahlreiche andere Sportarten ausgeübt: Seitenwagen-Polo, Miniauto-Rennen, Boxen, Speedway-Rennen und Kricket, und es fanden dort sogar Katzen- und Hundeschauen statt.

Juin 1938. Rodéo dans les jardins du Crystal Palace, Londres. Ces motocyclistes s'essaient à une nouvelle technique de glisse. Le parc accueillait des événements très divers : polo de side-cars, course de mini-voitures, tournois de boxe, de cricket et même concours de chats et chiens.

February 1938. A basketball training session for the
Catford Saints. The team were trained by Brigham
Young the Fifth, great-great-grandson of the founder
of the Mormon Church.

Februar 1938. Basketballtraining bei den Catford
Saints. Trainer der Mannschaft war Brigham Young
V., der Ururenkel des Gründers der Mormonensekte.

Février 1938. Séance d'entraînement pour l'équipe
de basket-ball des Catford Saints. Son entraîneur
était Brigham Young V, l'arrière arrière-petit-fils du
fondateur de l'Eglise mormone.

A little drop of the Irish. Jack Doyle, the Irish heavyweight, lies sprawled on the canvas after being knocked out by Eddie Phillips at White City, London, in 1939. Doyle was not a lucky boxer against Phillips. In a 1938 fight, he swung a punch at Phillips, missed, fell out of the ring, and was counted out.

Ein Schlag zuviel. Der irische Schwergewichtsboxer Jack Doyle liegt nach einem Knockout durch Eddie Phillips im Ring des Londoner Stadions White City, 1939. Doyle hatte gegen diesen Boxer kein Glück. 1938 holte er zum Schlag gegen Phillips aus, verfehlte ihn jedoch, stürzte aus dem Ring und wurde ausgezählt.

Un coup en trop. Jack Doyle, le poids lourd irlandais, étendu au sol après avoir été mis K. O. par Eddie Phillips au White City, Londres, 1939. Doyle n'a jamais eu de chance face à Phillips. En 1938, il balança un coup de poing à Phillips, le manqua, tomba du ring et fut disqualifié.

11. Children
Kinder
Les enfants

June 1939. Two young Jewish refugees from Germany at a porthole of
the liner *St Louis*. They had originally sailed to Miami, then to Lisbon.
In both places they were denied entry. Now they are staring at Antwerp.

Juni 1939. Zwei jüdische Flüchtlingskinder aus Deutschland schauen
aus einem Bullauge des Liniendampfers *St. Louis*. Ihre Reise führte
zuerst nach Miami, dann nach Lissabon – doch in beiden Häfen
verweigerte man ihnen die Aufnahme. Nun blicken sie zweifelnd auf
den Hafen von Antwerpen.

Juin 1939. Deux petits réfugiés juifs allemands regardent par le hublot
du *Saint-Louis*. Ils avaient d'abord mis le cap sur Miami puis Lisbonne,
où ils avaient été refoulés. Ils attendaient maintenant à Anvers.

11. Children
Kinder
Les enfants

Most adults look back on their childhood with fondness. Those who grew up in the Thirties are no exception. By modern standards it was a time of great freedom for children – there were woods to be explored, streams to be dammed, birds' nests to be plundered. They knew little of the restrictions placed on contemporary children, and nothing of the licence granted to contemporary teenagers. It was one last Indian summer of bucolic play before the winter of industrialization and urbanization closed in on us all.

Role models changed. Christopher Robin and his nursery toys gave way to child star Shirley Temple. Winnie-the-Pooh's poetry came second to Shirley's tap-dancing skills.

Schools were often places of fear, where punishment was summary and physical, and authority was traditional and unquestioned. Children passed this cruelty on to smaller children and to animals. For the rich and middle classes, although no less cruelly treated at their expensive schools, there were the consolations of wonderful toys: electric train sets, construction kits, pedal cars that were midget versions of the real thing, ponies that were real, and extravagantly beautiful doll's houses.

The poor often had to be content with empty tins, bits of wood, and recycled nails.

Die meisten Erwachsenen erinnern sich gerne an ihre Kindheit, auch die Menschen, die in den dreißiger Jahren aufwuchsen. Verglichen mit heutigen Maßstäben war es eine Zeit, in der die Kinder große Freiheit genossen – es galt, Wälder zu erforschen, Staudämme zu bauen und Vogelnester zu plündern. Sie kannten die Einschränkungen, die Kindern heute auferlegt werden, nur in bedingtem Maße und die Freiheit, die Teenager heute genießen, überhaupt nicht. In jener Zeit erlebten die Kinder den letzten Altweibersommer des freien Spielens in der Natur – bevor der Winter der Industrialisierung und Verstädterung hereinbrach.

Die Vorbilder der Kinder wandelten sich: Christopher Robin und seine Spielzeuggefährten wurden von dem Kinderstar Shirley Temple abgelöst. Reime von Puh, dem Bären, konnten mit Shirleys Steptanzeinlagen nicht mithalten.

In den Schulen regierte häufig die Angst, denn die schmerzhaften Bestrafungen erfolgten willkürlich. Die jeweiligen Autoritäten wurden dabei nicht in Frage gestellt. Viele Kinder übernahmen dieses grausame Verhalten von den Erwachsenen und gaben den Druck an kleinere Kinder und Tiere weiter. Die Kinder der gehobeneren und mittleren Schichten, denen auf ihren teuren Schulen nicht etwa eine sanftere Behandlung widerfuhr, suchten Trost in ihrem wunderbaren Spielzeug: in elektrischen Eisenbahnen, Baukästen, Tretautos, Miniaturausgaben der echten Wagen, Ponys und luxuriös ausgestatteten Puppenhäusern.

Die ärmeren Kinder mußten sich oft mit leeren Dosen, Holzresten und alten Nägeln als Spielzeug zufriedengeben.

La plupart des adultes ont gardé un souvenir attendri de leur enfance comme ceux qui grandirent dans les années trente. Par rapport aux critères actuels, les enfants disposaient de plus de temps libre – pour explorer les forêts, construire des digues, piller des nids d'oiseaux – et ne connurent ni les restrictions imposées aux enfants d'aujourd'hui ni la permissivité dont bénéficient les adolescents. Ce fut comme un long été indien, le dernier où l'on put jouer dehors avant l'arrivée d'une ère industrielle et urbaine qui renverrait tout le monde à l'intérieur.

Les références changèrent. Jean-Christophe et ses peluches cédèrent la place à l'enfant-vedette Shirley Temple, reléguant ainsi la poésie de Winnie l'Ourson à la deuxième place, derrière Shirley et ses claquettes.

L'école était un lieu qui inspirait la peur, où les punitions étaient primitives et physiques et où l'autorité s'exerçait sans faillir. Les enfants retournaient cette cruauté sur les plus petits qu'eux et les animaux. Dans les écoles privées, les enfants des classes aisées subissaient aussi des traitements cruels mais ils avaient, pour se consoler, de merveilleux jouets : des trains électriques, des jeux de mécano, des voitures à pédales ressemblant à des mini-voitures, des poneys en chair et en os et des maisons de poupées adorables.

Les pauvres devaient souvent se contenter de boîtes de conserve vides, de quelques bouts de bois de clous recyclés.

February 1936. Young demonstrators take part in a Popular Front march through Paris. Led by Léon Blum, this was the year the Popular Front was elected to power in France. It was an uneasy coalition of communists, liberals and socialists, united solely in their opposition to fascism.

Februar 1936. Junge Demonstranten beteiligen sich an einem Pariser Marsch der „Volksfront". Unter der Führung Léon Blums gewannen sie in jenem Jahr die französischen Wahlen. Weniger eine Partei als eine unbequeme Koalition von Kommunisten, Sozialisten und Liberalen, bestand ihr einziges gemeinsames Ziel im Widerstand gegen den Faschismus.

Février 1936. Des gamins à une manifestation du Front Populaire, Paris. Cette année-là, conduit par Léon Blum, le Front Populaire gagna les élections. La coalition fut difficile pour les communistes, libéraux et socialistes unis seulement dans leur opposition au fascisme.

October 1932. A group of young National
Socialists in Potsdam. The occasion was the
inaugural Reich Youth Convention of the party.

Oktober 1932. Junge Nationalsozialisten in
Potsdam. Anlaß für diese Parade war der Er-
öffnungskonvent der Reichsjugend der Partei.

Octobre 1932. Défilé de jeunes national-
socialistes à Postdam lors de l'inauguration
d'une fête de la Jeunesse du Reich, organisée
par leur parti.

Seven-year-old Jacqueline Loman addresses a class at Cheadle High School, near Manchester. Once a week her teacher gives a lesson on current affairs, after which the pupils discuss the chosen topic. This lesson had been on the subject of 'democracy and Hitlerism'.

Die siebenjährige Jacqueline Loman wendet sich an ihre Klassenkameraden in der High School von Cheadle bei Manchester. Einmal in der Woche wurden aktuelle Themen diskutiert. In dieser Stunde behandelten die Schüler „demokratische Grundsätze und Hitlers Politik".

Jacqueline Loman, sept ans, prend la parole devant sa classe à l'école de Cheadle, près de Manchester. Une fois par semaine, la maîtresse donnait une leçon sur des questions d'actualité puis les élèves en discutaient. Ce jour-là, la leçon portait sur la « démocratie et Hitler ».

Meanwhile, a couple of hundred miles away... A German teacher gives
a lesson to his class on the importance of Danzig (now Gdansk, Poland), in
the Polish Corridor that separated East Prussia from the rest of Germany.

Zur gleichen Zeit, nur wenige hundert Kilometer entfernt... Ein deutscher
Lehrer hält eine Unterrichtsstunde über die politische Bedeutung
Danzigs (das heutige Gdansk in Polen), das im polnischen Korridor lag
und Ostpreußen vom übrigen Gebiet Deutschlands trennte.

Pendant ce temps, à quelques centaines de kilomètres de là...
Un instituteur allemand donnait une leçon sur l'importance de Dantzig
(aujourd'hui Gdansk, Pologne) et du couloir qui séparait l'est de la
Prusse du reste de l'Allemagne.

June 1935. Violet
Hutchinson (aged 8)
and Betty Putt
(aged 7) rehearse a
back garden ballet in
Poplar, East London.

Juni 1935. Violet
Hutchinson
(8 Jahre) und Betty
Putt (7 Jahre)
proben ein
Hinterhofballett in
Poplar, Ost-London.

Juin 1935. Violet
Hutchinson (huit
ans) et Betty Putt
(sept ans) répètent
un ballet dans le
jardin d'une maison
de Poplar dans l'Est
de Londres.

August 1934.
Outward Bound!
A home-made raft
takes to the water at
the popular seaside
resort of Frinton-on-
Sea, Essex.

August 1934. Setzt
die Segel! Ein
selbstgebautes Floß
wird in dem
beliebten Badeort
Frinton-on-Sea,
Essex, zu Wasser
gelassen.

Août 1934. En avant
toutes ! Un radeau
fait maison est mis à
l'eau à Frinton-on-
Sea, une station
balnéaire de l'Essex,
alors très en vogue.

October 1938.
What the well-dressed
schoolgirl is wearing
– a cameo of village
life in England.

Oktober 1938.
Das trägt man jetzt
als modebewußte
Schülerin – eine
Momentaufnahme
englischen
Dorflebens.

Octobre 1938.
Voici la tenue d'une
écolière bien habillée
– saynète de vie
ordinaire dans un
village anglais.

May 1934. Girls from the Woodford County High School collect specimens for their aquarium from a pond in Epping Forest, London. It was a time when schools insisted that every schoolchild wore a hat or a cap.

Mai 1934. Schülerinnen der staatlichen High School von Woodford sammeln im Londoner Stadtwald von Epping kleine Tiere für ihr Aquarium. Damals gehörten Hut oder Mütze zur allgemeinen Schuluniform.

Mai 1934. Etang de la forêt d'Epping, Londres. Des élèves du lycée de Woodford County tentent d'attraper des poissons pour leur aquarium. A cette époque, les élèves devaient tous porter un chapeau ou une casquette.

September 1937. The joys of a fight with wet sand, Lavernock, South Wales. The photograph was probably taken at a weekend, as most children would have been back at school by that date. If so, these are almost certainly local children, from Barry or Penarth.

September 1937. Die Freuden einer Schlammschlacht, Lavernock, Südwales. Diese Aufnahme entstand wahrscheinlich an einem Wochenende, da für die meisten Kinder die Sommerferien bereits vorüber waren. Vermutlich stammen diese Kinder aus der Umgebung, aus Barry oder Penarth.

Septembre 1937. Les joies de la lutte au sable mouillé, Lavernock, sud du Pays de Galles. Ce cliché fut certainement pris un week-end car, à cette date-là, la plupart des enfants avaient recommencé l'école. Ces enfants viennent probablement d'un village voisin, Barry ou Penarth.

Firemen turn their hoses on children, London 1935. This is
not riot control – the city was sweltering in a heat wave that
summer. In those days, firemen had time to play with children.

Londoner Feuerwehrleute richten ihre Wasserschläuche auf
Kinder, um bei der großen Hitzewelle von 1935 für eine
Erfrischung zu sorgen. Damals hatte die Feuerwehr noch Zeit,
mit Kindern zu spielen.

Enfants arrosés avec des tuyaux d'incendie, Londres, 1935.
Aucune émeute en vue. Cet été-là, la ville fut écrasée par une
vague de chaleur et les pompiers avaient assez de temps pour
jouer avec les enfants.

December 1937. A small boy waits for the school milk to thaw by the radiators. The daily arrival of school milk, the clatter of the crate, the rattle of the bottles, was the high point of the day for many children.

Dezember 1937. Ein kleiner Junge wartet neben der Heizung darauf, daß die gefrorene Schulmilch auftaut. Die tägliche Lieferung der Milch, die sich durch das Geklapper der Kisten und das Klirren der Flaschen ankündigte, war für viele Kinder der Höhepunkt des Tages.

Décembre 1937. Un petit garçon attend que le lait dégèle. La livraison du lait à l'école – dans un bruit de bouteilles qui s'entrechoquaient et de cageots qui crissaient – était pour bien des enfants le moment le plus attendu de la journée.

Another summer, another heat wave in London – this time in August 1939. The blocks of ice were almost certainly destined for a fishmonger's, at a time when freezers or chilled cabinets were rarely seen.

Auch im August 1939 gab es wieder eine Hitzewelle in London. Die Eisblöcke waren vermutlich für einen Fischhändler bestimmt, da Gefriertruhen und Kühlschränke noch eine Seltenheit waren.

Autre été, autre vague de chaleur à Londres, cette fois-ci en août 1939. Ce bloc de glace était sans aucun doute destiné à un marchand de poisson car, à cette époque, les congélateurs ou les armoires frigorifiques étaient rares.

Harrow schoolboys
line up for the 'Bill'
(call-over) at the
start of the School
Speech Day, 1935.

Schüler der Privat-
schule in Harrow
stellen sich für den
Aufruf zu Beginn
ihrer Schulfeier an,
1935.

Des élèves de l'école
privée de Harrow se
mettent en rang
pour l'appel avant la
cérémonie scolaire,
1935.

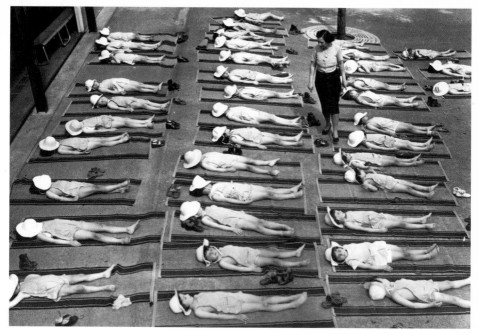

Lying down on the job – pupils at a progressive school in Paris, April 1939. Much emphasis was placed on the importance of rest and fresh air in the development of children in the Thirties. Most infants were supposed to lie down after midday dinner.

Schlafen im Dienst – Schüler einer fortschrittlichen Pariser Schule, April 1939. Um die kindliche Entwicklung zu fördern, legte man in den dreißiger Jahren großen Wert auf Ruhe und frische Luft. Die meisten Grundschulkinder mußten nach dem Essen in der Schule einen Mittagsschlaf halten.

Travailler en dormant – élèves d'une école progressiste à Paris, avril 1939. Dans les années trente, on insistait beaucoup sur l'importance du repos et de l'air frais pour le développement de l'enfant. La plupart des enfant devaient faire la sieste après le déjeuner.

July 1931.
Hopscotch in a
school playground.
The poet Laurie Lee
wrote, 'Old boots,
ragged stockings,
torn trousers and
skirts went skidding
around me...'
– *Cider with Rosie.*

Juli 1931. Himmel-
und-Hölle auf einem
Schulhof. Laurie Lee
schrieb in *Cider with
Rosie*: „Alte Stiefel,
ausgefranste
Strümpfe und
zerrissene Hosen
und Röcke wirbelten
um mich herum."

Juillet 1931. Marelle
dans un préau. Le
poète Laurie Lee
écrivait dans *Cider
with Rosie* : « Autour
de moi tournoyaient
en glissant des
vieilles bottes, des
collants en
lambeaux, des
pantalons et des
jupes déchirés. »

June 1938. A giant globe in the playground of a school in Paris. In just a couple of years the globe would be considerably out of date.

Juni 1938. Eine riesige Weltkugel auf dem Pausenhof einer Pariser Schule. Nur wenige Jahre später sollte dieser Globus nicht mehr auf dem aktuellsten Stand sein.

Juin 1938. Une planisphère géante dans le préau d'une école à Paris. Quelques années plus tard, elle serait en grande partie périmée.

London, 1937. Queueing for the Saturday morning matinée outside a Plaistow cinema. The feature serial was *Flash Gordon*. A contemporary account described how the children rushed out of the cinema at the end of the show, and gave 'hell to the policeman on duty in the street outside'.

London, 1937. Schlangestehen für die Samstagmorgen-Vorstellung in einem Kino in Plaistow. Auf dem Programm stand ein Film des Serienhelden *Flash Gordon*. Zeitgenössischen Aufzeichnungen zufolge stürmten die Kinder nach dem Film aus dem Gebäude und machten „dem Polizisten, der vor dem Kino Dienst hatte, die Hölle heiß".

Londres, 1937. Queue pour la séance du samedi matin devant un cinéma de Plaistow. Au programme, *Flash Gordon*. Des témoins de l'époque racontent qu'après le film les enfants sortaient du cinéma en courant et « faisant enrager le policier de service dans la rue ».

Wonder on wheels, Oxford, March 1933. Roller-skating
became a craze in the Thirties, with clubs and rinks all
over Europe and the United States.

Ein Wunder auf Rollen, Oxford, März 1933. Roll-
schuhlaufen wurde in den dreißiger Jahren zur großen
Mode. Überall in Europa und den Vereinigten Staaten
wurden Sportvereine und Rollschuhbahnen geöffnet.

Merveille à roulettes, Oxford, mars 1933. Le patin à
roulettes fit fureur dans les années trente. Des clubs et des
pistes s'ouvrirent partout en Europe et aux Etats-Unis.

12. All human life
Menschliches, Allzumenschliches
Petits et grands événements

May 1939. Mr and Mrs Townsend of Stanton Harcourt, Oxfordshire, celebrate their golden wedding anniversary. They announced that they were 'still as much in love as ever'. When they married, radio, powered flight, the motor car and the cinema did not exist.

Mai 1939. Das Ehepaar Townsend aus Stanton Harcourt, Oxfordshire, feiert seine goldene Hochzeit. Es verkündete stolz, daß die Zeit ihre Liebe nicht geschmälert hätte. Als sie den Bund fürs Leben schlossen, gab es noch kein Radio, keine Motorflugzeuge, keine Autos und kein Kino.

Mai 1939. M. et Mme Townsend de Stanton Harcourt, Oxfordshire, célèbrent leurs noces d'or. Ils déclarèrent qu'ils étaient toujours aussi amoureux l'un de l'autre. A leur mariage, la radio, l'avion à moteur, l'automobile et le cinéma n'existaient pas encore.

12. All human life
Menschliches, Allzumenschliches
Petits et grands événements

There was still plenty of time and space for eccentrics and oddities to thrive in the Thirties. The programme at an average music hall would include at least one novelty act, every village had its 'character', and freak shows were to be found in most travelling fairs. A notable eccentric, the defrocked Vicar of Stiffkey, was killed while lion taming at Skegness in 1932.

Disasters made the news. A hundred and twenty people died in an earthquake in California in 1933. Millions were made homeless by floods in Louisiana in 1937. The liner *Morro Castle* caught fire in September 1934, and 130 people died in the flames. Seventy-three sailors of the US Navy were drowned when the airship *Akron* crashed into the sea in 1933. As many people were killed on the roads as today, when there is ten times the volume of traffic.

It was easier to pull the wool over people's eyes. A teenage girl from the Isle of Man managed to persuade her parents, the newspapers and a credulous public that she owned a talking ferret. Count Victor Lustig fraudulently sold the Eiffel Tower for scrap. Hans van Meegeren began his successful career painting fake 'old masters'.

The motto of the Thirties could well have been W C Fields' misanthropic saying: 'Never give a sucker an even break.'

In den dreißiger Jahren gab es noch genügend Freiräume, in denen sich Exzentriker und Absonderlichkeiten entwickeln konnten. Jedes Varietétheater hatte mindestens eine Neuheiten-Nummer im Programm, jedes kleine Nest besaß seinen eigenen bizarren Dorfbewohner und fast jeder Jahrmarkt bot eine Monstrositätenschau. Der des Priesteramts enthobene Pfarrer von Stiffkey, ein sehr bekannter Exzentriker, kam 1932 bei dem Versuch, einen Löwen zu zähmen, in Skegness ums Leben.

Katastrophen machten Schlagzeilen: 1933 starben einhundertzwanzig Menschen bei einem

Erdbeben in Kalifornien. Millionen Menschen wurden obdachlos, als Louisiana 1937 von schweren Überschwemmungen heimgesucht wurde. Im September 1934 brach auf dem Liniendampfer *Morro Castle* ein Feuer aus, bei dem 130 Passagiere ums Leben kamen. 73 amerikanische Marinesoldaten ertranken, als das Luftschiff *Akron* im Jahre 1933 ins Meer stürzte. Und auf den Straßen starben damals ebenso viele Menschen wie heute, obwohl das Verkehrsaufkommen mittlerweile auf das Zehnfache angestiegen ist.

Es war noch einfach, die Menschen hinters Licht zu führen. Einem jungen Mädchen von der Isle of Man gelang es, nicht nur seine Eltern, sondern auch die Zeitungen und eine leichtgläubige Öffentlichkeit davon zu überzeugen, daß sie ein sprechendes Frettchen besaß. Graf Victor Lustig verkaufte bei einer Betrügerei den Eiffelturm, um ihn verschrotten zu lassen. Und Hans van Meegeren machte erfolgreich Karriere als Maler von Bildern „alter Meister".

Das Motto der dreißiger Jahre hätte W. C. Fields' menschenfeindlicher Ausspruch sein können: „Gib einem Narren nie eine faire Chance."

Dans les années trente, l'insolite avait encore de beaux jours devant lui. Presque chaque music-hall proposait au moins un numéro nouveau dans son programme, chaque village avait son fou et les monstres étaient chose courante dans les foires ambulantes. En 1932, un excentrique réputé, le vicaire défroqué de Stiffkey, fut tué à Skegness alors qu'il tentait d'apprivoiser un lion.

Les désastres faisaient la une des journaux. En 1933, cent vingt personnes furent tuées dans un tremblement de terre en Californie. Des millions de personnes se retrouvèrent sans abri après les inondations de 1937 en Louisiane. Le paquebot *Morro Castle* prit feu en septembre 1934 et 130 personnes y trouvèrent la mort. En 1933, 73 marins de la flotte américaine furent noyés dans l'accident causé par le dirigeable *Akron* tombé en mer. Le nombre de personnes tuées sur les routes était aussi élevé qu'aujourd'hui, alors qu'il y avait dix fois moins de circulation.

Les gens étaient d'une grande crédulité. Une adolescente de l'île de Man réussit à faire croire à ses parents, aux journaux et à tout un public naïf que son furet savait parler. Le comte Victor Lustig vendit frauduleusement la Tour Eiffel à une casse. Hans van Meegeren commençait à avoir du succès avec ses reproductions d'anciens tableaux de maître.

Le slogan des années trente aurait pu s'inspirer d'une citation de W. C. Fields, misanthrope confirmé : « Ne donnez jamais une deuxième chance à un gogo. »

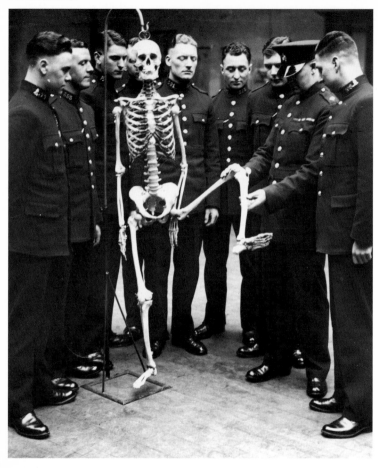

April 1937.
Members of the
Lancashire Police
receive an unlikely
looking first-aid
lesson at Lancaster
Castle.

April 1937.
Polizisten aus
Lancashire erhalten
auf Lancaster Castle
ungewöhnlichen
Unterricht in erster
Hilfe.

Avril 1937.
Des membres de la
police de Lancashire
reçoivent une leçon
de premier secours
au château de
Lancaster, pour les
moins insolite.

Dabbling with the spirit world at a seance in Berlin,
1930. In the Thirties, belief in psychic phenomena
was probably more widespread than it is today.

Auf Tuchfühlung mit dem Jenseits bei einer spiriti-
stischen Sitzung in Berlin, 1930. Der Glaube an
übernatürliche Kräfte war in den dreißiger Jahren
sogar noch verbreiteter als heute.

Séance de spiritisme à Berlin, 1930. Dans les
années trente, la croyance dans les phénomènes
surnaturels était sans doute plus répandue
qu'aujourd'hui.

December 1930. Professor Tindall demonstrates the effect of 'electrification'
on hair. The professor, wearing a special electric mask, was speaking
to schoolchildren at a Christmas lecture at the Royal Institute in London.

Dezember 1930. Mit Hilfe einer speziell konstruierten elektrischen Maske
demonstriert Professor Tindall einigen Schülern die Wirkung der
„Elektrifizierung" der Haare. Das Experiment war Teil seines Weihnachts-
vortrages im Londoner Royal Institute.

Décembre 1930. Les effets de l'électrification sur la chevelure du professeur
Tindall, recouvert d'un masque spécial, lors d'une conférence donnée aux
écoliers à l'Institut Royal de Londres pour Noël.

Theory into practice
– a barber cuts a
customer's hair that
has been charged
with static electricity,
1930.

… und hier die
praktische An-
wendung. Ein
Friseur schneidet
einem Kunden sein
mit statischer
Elektrizität geladenes
Haar, 1930.

De la théorie à la
pratique – un barbier
coupe les cheveux
d'un client chargé
d'électricité statique,
1930.

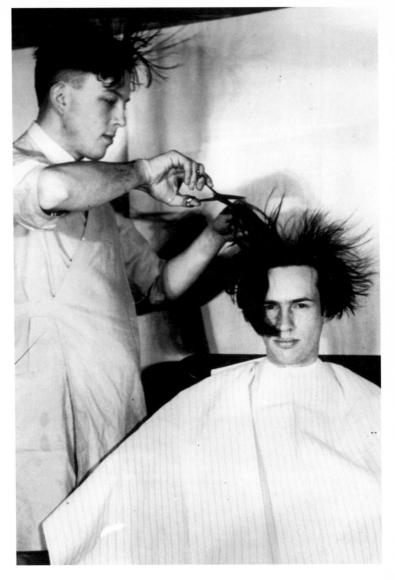

Extending a helping hand, London 1934. A motorist uses a newly
designed 'dummy hand' to signal the direction in which he intends to
drive. It was supposed to ease traffic flow. It was not a success.

Eine hilfreiche Hand, London, 1934. Die Vorläufer von Blinkern, die
die Fahrtrichtung anzeigen, waren solche ausklappbaren „Hände".
Sie sollte den Verkehrsfluß erleichtern, waren aber leider kein Erfolg.

La main tendue, Londres, 1934. Un automobiliste utilise une main
factice pour signaler un changement de direction. Ce nouveau type
d'indicateur, conçu pour faciliter la circulation, ne fut pas un succès.

Extending the neck, London, 1935.
Three giraffe-necked women from Burma
ask directions from a London policeman.

Lange Hälse, London, 1935. Drei Frauen
aus Burma in Landestracht fragen einen
Polizisten nach dem Weg.

Haut perchées, Londres, 1935. Trois
femmes-girafes de Birmanie demandent
leur chemin à un policier londonien.

November 1930. Waiters serve construction workers on the Empire State Building in New York. Pictures of such daredevil action were great publicity, but it is unlikely that the men in this photograph were real waiters.

November 1930. Zwei Kellner servieren Bauarbeitern ein Festmahl auf dem Empire State Building in New York. Solche todesmutigen Aufnahmen hatten eine große Werbewirkung. Es ist allerdings anzunehmen, daß diese Kellner normalerweise kein Essen servierten.

Novembre 1930. Des garçons de café servent des ouvriers sur l'Empire State Building à New York. Des photographies aussi audacieuses que celle-ci faisaient beaucoup de publicité mais il est peu vraisemblable qu'il s'agisse de vrais serveurs.

A band of midgets greet the son of the Sultan of Morocco during his
visit to the Paris Exhibition, 1930. The Sultan's son seems bewildered
but the midgets are taking it in their stride.

Eine Gruppe von Kleinwüchsigen begrüßt den Sohn des Sultans von
Marokko während seines Besuchs der Pariser Ausstellung im Jahre
1930. Dem kleinen Sultan steht die Überraschung förmlich im Gesicht
geschrieben, doch die Grüßenden nehmen das Staunen gelassen hin.

Un groupe de nains accueillent le fils du sultan du Maroc en visite
à l'Exposition de Paris, 1930. Le fils du sultan a l'air étonné mais les
nains font comme si de rien n'était.

Robert Wadlow of Illinois
being measured for a jacket,
1939. At 8 feet 11 inches
(2.7 metres) Wadlow was the
tallest man in the world.
He died the following year,
aged 22.

Ein Schneider nimmt Maß
bei Robert Wadlow aus Illinois,
1939. Mit seinen 2,70 Metern
war Wadlow unbestritten
der größte Mann der Welt.
Er verstarb ein Jahr später im
Alter von 22 Jahren.

Mesures pour une veste. D'une
taille de 2,7 mètres, Robert
Wadlow, originaire de l'Illinois,
était l'homme le plus grand du
monde. Il mourut l'année
suivante, à l'âge de 22 ans.

1933. A true British eccentric, Captain Pfeiffer, is photographed at the London Zoological Society, offering a biscuit to one of the giraffes.

1933. Ein wahrer britischer Exzentriker. Captain Pfeiffer bietet im Londoner Zoologischen Garten einer Giraffe einen Keks an.

1933. Un vrai excentrique britannique. Le capitaine Pfeiffer est photographié offrant un gâteau à une des girafes du zoo de Londres.

1934. Captain Pfeiffer, still at the London Zoological Society, puts his hand inside the mouth of Joan the hippopotamus. Sadly, there are no pictures from 1935.

1934. Captain Pfeiffer legt vertrauensvoll seine Hand in das Maul der Nilpferddame Joan. Die Aufnahme aus dem folgenden Jahr ist nicht erhalten …

1934. Le capitaine Pfeiffer, toujours au zoo de Londres, met sa main dans la gueule de Joan l'hippopotame. Aucun cliché ne permet de savoir ce qu'il entreprit l'année suivante, c'est dommage.

December 1938. Staff at Spiers and Pond's poultry department prepare turkeys for the Christmas market, London. The diplomat Harold Nicholson noted in his diary, 'It has been a bad year. A foul year. Next year will be worse.'

Dezember 1938. Angestellte der Geflügelabteilung von Spiers and Pond's bereiten Truthähne für das Londoner Weihnachtsgeschäft vor. „Es war ein schlechtes Jahr, ein ganz übles Jahr, und das nächste Jahr wird noch schlimmer werden", notierte der Diplomat Harold Nicholson in seinem Tagebuch.

Décembre 1938. Des employés du département volailles chez Spiers and Pond préparent des dindes pour le marché de Noël, Londres. Extrait du journal du diplomate Harold Nicholson : « Ce fut une mauvaise année. Une année infecte. L'année prochaine sera pire. »

One of the first arrivals at the Grand International Poultry, Pigeon and Rabbit Show at Crystal Palace, November 1932.

Einer der ersten Ankömmlinge auf der Großen Internationalen Geflügel-, Tauben- und Kaninchenschau, die im Londoner Kristallpalast stattfand, November 1932.

Une des premières arrivées à la Grande Exposition Internationale de volailles, pigeons et lapins au Crystal Palace, novembre 1932.

Unlikely Friendships, One. An alligator gets a
wash-and-brush-up at a zoo, 12 April 1935.

Ungewöhnliche Freundschaften, Nr. 1.
Ein Alligator im Zoo unterzieht sich seiner
täglichen Morgentoilette, 12. April 1935.

Amitié inattendue, scène une. Brin de toilette
pour un alligator du zoo, 12 avril 1935.

Unlikely Friendships, Two. Mr Egbert takes his five-year-old lion for a ride on the Wall of Death at Mitcham Fair near London, 1935. One assumes the couple were part of the fair – it seems hardly likely that they just turned up for the ride.

Ungewöhnliche Freundschaften, Nr. 2. Mr. Egbert und sein fünfjähriger Löwe drehen 1935 auf dem Jahrmarkt von Mitcham bei London eine gemeinsame Runde in der „Todeswand". Es ist anzunehmen, daß das Paar zu den Schaustellern gehörte und nicht nur vorbeikam, um sich zu vergnügen.

Amitié inattendue, scène deux. M. Egbert emmène son lion, âgé de cinq ans, faire un tour sur le « mur de la mort » à la foire de Mitcham près de Londres, 1935. Ce couple faisait sûrement partie de la foire – il est peu vraisemblable qu'il soit là par hasard.

In the year following the 1929 collapse of the Wall Street stock market,
it was very difficult to recruit reliable staff, and families were often
forced to employ the most unlikely-looking cooks, maids and chauffeurs.

Der Börsenkrach von 1929 und seine Auswirkungen machten es
zunehmend schwieriger, zuverlässiges Personal zu finden. Bald waren
Familien gezwungen, die merkwürdigsten Köche, Hausmädchen und
Chauffeure einzustellen.

Après l'effondrement de la bourse de Wall Street en 1929, il devint très
difficile de trouver des domestiques de confiance et les familles furent
souvent obligées de faire appel aux cuisiniers, domestiques et chauffeurs
les plus inattendus.

An ostrich, with its
neck well bandaged
against the cold, sets
out to pull a light
cart, 1930.

Ein Strauß, dem zum
Schutz vor der Kälte
eine Art Rollkragen
übergestülpt wurde,
setzt an, einen
leichten Wagen zu
ziehen, 1930.

Une autruche dont le
cou est protégé du
froid par un bandage
est prête pour la
course, 1930.

Unarmed combat. The Swiss-born jujitsu master, Adolf Tobler, sets out
to demonstrate some new holds to members of the Berlin Police, 1935.
History, alas, does not record what happened to Monsieur Tobler.

Unbewaffneter Kampf. Der gebürtige Schweizer und Jujutsu-Meister
Adolf Tobler zeigt Berliner Polizisten einige neue Griffe, 1935. Über
sein weiteres Schicksal ist nichts bekannt.

Combat sans armes. Adolf Tobler, le maître du jiu-jitsu d'origine suisse,
enseigne de nouvelles prises à des policiers berlinois, 1935. L'histoire,
hélas, n'a conservé aucune trace de M. Tobler.

Armed combat. Detectives test bullet-proof vests at very close range, 1930. What happened to the bullet-proof vest, or the man inside it, remains a mystery, though one can assume that their futures were inextricably linked.

Bewaffneter Kampf. Kriminalbeamte beim Test von kugelsicheren Westen aus nächster Nähe, 1930. Wie die getestete Weste abschnitt, und ob der Mann, der sie trug, das Experiment überlebte, ist nicht überliefert.

Combat armé. Des policiers tirent à bout portant sur un homme vêtu d'un gilet pare-balles, 1930. Qu'est-il advenu du gilet pare-balles ou plutôt de l'homme qui le portait, nul ne le sait. Tout dépendit du succès de ces essais.

A hoard of elephant tusks in a London warehouse, 1930. There were then no restrictions on the ivory trade. It was simply one of the thousands of products that poured into London from the far-flung British Empire.

Eine mit sorgfältig geschichteten Stoßzähnen gefüllte Londoner Lagerhalle, 1930. Zu jener Zeit waren dem Elfenbeinhandel keine Grenzen gesetzt. Das „weiße Gold" gehörte zu Tausenden von Waren, die aus dem großen Britischen Weltreich nach London verschifft wurden.

Stock de défenses d'éléphants dans un entrepôt à Londres, 1930. Le commerce de l'ivoire n'était soumis à aucune restriction. L'ivoire était un des milliers de produits importés à Londres des quatre coins de l'Empire britannique.

The charnel-house beneath the church of St Martin-in-the Fields,
Trafalgar Square, London, 1936. The vaults had been opened up prior
to their demolition. The crypt of the church became an air-raid shelter
during the war.

Das Beinhaus unterhalb der Kirche von St Martin-in-the-Fields am
Trafalgar Square, London, 1936. Es wurde nach seiner Öffnung aufgelöst
und die Krypta der Kirche wurde im Krieg als Luftschutzbunker genutzt.

Ossuaire de l'église de St-Martin-in-the-Fields, Trafalgar Square, Londres,
1936. Les caveaux furent ouverts au public avant leur démolition et la
crypte de l'église servit d'abri antiaérien durant la guerre.

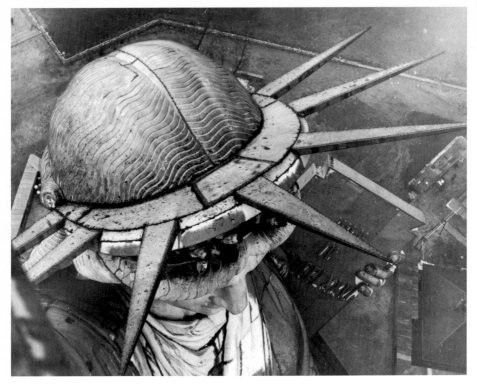

Symbolic woman, one. The head of the Statue of
Liberty, New York Harbour, 1930. The statue was
originally made in France in the 1880s.

Symbolische Frau, Nr. 1. Der Kopf der Freiheitsstatue
im New Yorker Hafen, 1930. Die Statue wurde
ursprünglich in Frankreich in den Jahren 1880 gebaut.

Femme symbole, scène une. La tête de la Statue de la
Liberté, port de New York, 1930. La statue avait été
fabriquée en France dans les années 1880.

Symbolic woman,
two. This giant
Britannia was carved
from stone by
Monsieur Desruelles
in 1937, to
commemorate
the British
Expeditionary Force
of 1914.

Symbolische Frau,
Nr. 2. Diese
gigantische Britannia
aus Stein schuf der
Bildhauer Monsieur
Desruelles 1937 zum
Gedenken an das
Britische Expedi-
tionskorps von
1914.

Femme symbole,
scène deux. Cette
Britannia géante fut
sculptée dans la
pierre par Monsieur
Desruelles en 1937
pour une com-
mémoration en
l'honneur du corps
expéditionnaire
britannique de 1914.

30 November 1936. The destruction of the Crystal Palace. The huge palace of glass and iron went up in flames, probably as a result of a burning cigarette being left in a paint store. The glow could be seen from 50 miles (80 kilometres) away. Molten glass ran down the streets of south London. But no one was killed.

30. November 1936. Die Zerstörung des Londoner Kristallpalastes. Die Ursache des verheerenden Brandes, der das gewaltige Gebäude aus Gußeisen und Glas vernichtete, war vermutlich eine brennende Zigarette gewesen, die jemand in einem Farblager vergessen hatte. Das Feuer war noch 80 Kilometer weit entfernt sichtbar. Flüssiges Glas rann durch die Straßen Süd-Londons. Glücklicherweise kam niemand bei dem Unglück ums Leben.

30 novembre 1936. Le Crystal Palace, gigantesque palais de verre et de fer, fut la proie des flammes. Le feu, probablement causé par une cigarette restée allumée dans un magasin de peintures, était visible jusqu'à 80 kilomètres de là. Le verre fondu se répandit dans les rues du sud de Londres. Il n'y eut aucune victime.

6 May 1937. The *Hindenburg* disaster at Lakehurst, New Jersey. The airship was completing its flight from Frankfurt with 97 people on board. Three hundred feet (100 metres) above ground it suddenly burst into flames. Thirty three people died and many more were injured.

6. Mai 1937. Das Ende der *Hindenburg* in Lakehurst, New Jersey. Das Luftschiff kam mit 97 Passagieren an Bord aus Frankfurt, als es am Ende seines Fluges in 100 Metern Höhe plötzlich in Flammen aufging. Dieses Unglück forderte 33 Tote und eine große Zahl von Verletzten.

6 mai 1937. La catastrophe du *Hindenburg* à Lakehurst, New Jersey. Le dirigeable achevait son vol en provenance de Francfort avec 97 passagers à son bord. Il prit soudain feu, à 100 mètres au-dessus du sol. Trente-trois personnes furent tuées et bien plus encore furent blessées.

13. Heading for war
Vorbereitung auf den Krieg
En marche vers la guerre

February 1939. Women workers at a factory in Southend, England, practising their gas-mask drill. Gas masks were distributed to the British public long before the start of the war. They smelt of rubber and made you feel sick – but that was better than being gassed.

Februar 1939. Arbeiterinnen den Einsatz von Gasmasken in einer Fabrik in Southend England. Schon lange vor Kriegsbeginn wurden an die britische Bevölkerung Gasmasken ausgegeben. Sie rochen stark nach Gummi und verursachten Übelkeit – alles jedoch besser, als an einer Gasvergiftung zu sterben.

Février 1939. Séance d'entraînement pour les ouvrières d'une usine de Southend, Angleterre. Ces masques à gaz furent distribués à la population britannique bien avant le début de la guerre. Ils sentaient le caoutchouc et donnaient envie de vomir, mais mieux valait ça que mourir asphyxié.

13. Heading for war
Vorbereitung auf den Krieg
En marche vers la guerre

Sixty years or more later, the debate still continues as to who should be blamed for World War II. Was it Clemenceau and Lloyd George, for the punitive peace terms they inflicted on Germany after World War I? Was it the Weimar Republic, for its seemingly easy-going approach to the massive problems of the Twenties? Was it the fault of those who gave way to Hitler's demands? Should Woodrow Wilson and the United States not have turned their backs on Europe in 1919? Was the weak dithering of the League of Nations responsible?

Whoever was to blame, the accelerating progression was clear for all to see. In March 1938, Nazis troops entered Austria, proclaiming the Anschluss (annexation). Seven months later they moved into Czechoslovakia's Sudetenland, as Hitler announced, 'Thus we begin our march into the great German future.' By March 1939, they were in Prague.

Chamberlain did his feeble best at Munich, but by then sandbags were being filled, shelters were being built, and every nation in Europe – save Switzerland – was stockpiling weapons.

The final steps were taken in August. Troops mobilized in Poland, France requisitioned her railways, Britain closed the Mediterranean and the Baltic to British merchant ships.

The following month, the German army crossed the Polish frontier.

Selbst 60 Jahre danach nimmt die Diskussion kein Ende, wer für den Zweiten Weltkrieg verantwortlich war. Waren es Clemenceau und Lloyd George, die Deutschland nach dem Ersten Weltkrieg extreme Friedensbedingungen auferlegt hatten? Oder war es die Weimarer Republik, die die großen Probleme der zwanziger Jahre scheinbar auf die leichte Schulter genommen hatte? Lag der Fehler bei denjenigen, die Hitlers Forderungen nachgegeben hatten? Hätten Woodrow Wilson und die Vereinigten Staaten Europa 1919 nicht im Stich lassen dürfen? Oder fehlte dem Völkerbund die nötige Entschlossenheit?

Wer auch immer der Schuldige war, die weitere Entwicklung konnte nicht aufgehalten werden. Im März 1938 marschierten die Nationalsozialisten in Österreich ein und proklamierten den Anschluß an das Deutsche Reich. Sieben Monate später zogen die Soldaten ins tschechische Sudetenland ein, während Hitler verkündete: „So beginnen wir unseren Marsch in die großdeutsche Zukunft." Im März 1939 hielten die Truppen bereits Einzug in Prag.

Der englische Außenminister Chamberlain versuchte zwar in München sein Möglichstes zu tun, doch zu diesem Zeitpunkt wurden bereits Sandsäcke gefüllt und Luftschutzbunker errichtet. Jeder europäische Staat – mit Ausnahme der Schweiz – legte Waffenarsenale an.

Die letzten Vorbereitungen erfolgten schließlich im August des Jahres. In Polen wurden Truppen mobilisiert, Frankreich requirierte seine Eisenbahnen und Großbritannien verwehrte britischen Handelsschiffen die Passage durch das Mittelmeer und die Ostsee.

Im darauffolgenden Monat überquerte die deutsche Wehrmacht die polnische Grenze.

Près de 60 ans plus tard, le débat se poursuit : qui furent les responsables de la Seconde Guerre mondiale ? Etaient-ce Clémenceau et Lloyd George qui infligèrent à l'Allemagne des conditions de paix punitives ? La République de Weimar qui traita avec trop de légèreté les graves problèmes des années vingt ? Woodrow Wilson et les Etats-Unis qui tournèrent le dos à l'Europe en 1919 ? Ou encore la Société des Nations qui manqua de fermeté ?

Quels que furent les responsables, la machine s'emballait et chacun en était conscient. En mars 1938, les soldats nazis pénétrèrent en Autriche, proclamant l'Anschluss (l'attachement au IIIᵉ Reich). Sept mois plus tard, ils annexaient les territoires sudètes de la Tchécoslovaquie. Comme l'avait annoncé Hitler, « Ainsi débute notre marche pour une future grande Allemagne. » En mars 1939, les Allemands étaient à Prague.

A Munich, Chamberlain fit au mieux, mais déjà chaque nation d'Europe, excepté la Suisse, commençait à remplir des sacs de sable, à construire des abris à stocker des armes.

Les dernières mesures furent décidées en août. Des troupes étaient mobilisées en Pologne, la France réquisitionna ses chemins de fer et la Grande-Bretagne ferma la Méditerranée et la Baltique à la marine marchande britannique.

Un mois plus tard, l'armée allemande franchissait la frontière polonaise.

March 1936. German troops reoccupy the Rhineland. The
move was a violation of the Locarno Pact, but the League
of Nations, and the international community, did nothing.

März 1936. Deutsche Truppen besetzen das Rheinland
und verstoßen somit gegen den Vertrag von Locarno. Aber
weder der Völkerbund noch die internationale Gemein-
schaft reagierten darauf.

Mars 1936. Soldats allemands en Rhénanie. Cette
manœuvre était une violation du pacte de Locarno mais ni
la Société des Nations ni la communauté internationale,
n'intervinrent.

October 1938. Sudeten Germans cheer Adolf Hitler's entry into Carlsbad (now Karlovy Vary, Czech Republic). 'In that case,' said Churchill, 'we shall have war.' But Chamberlain disappointed him, and Churchill had to wait another year.

Oktober 1938. Sudetendeutsche jubeln Adolf Hitler bei dessen Einzug in Karlsbad (heute Karlovy Vary, Tschechische Republik) zu. „In diesem Fall", erklärte Churchill, „ist ein Krieg unvermeidbar." Doch Außenminister Chamberlain widersetzte sich ihm, so daß der Krieg erst ein Jahr später ausbrach.

Octobre 1938. Des Sudètes allemands saluent l'entrée d'Adolf Hitler dans Carlsbad (aujourd'hui Karlovy Vary, République Tchèque). « Dans ce cas », déclara Churchill, « la guerre est imminente ». Mais Chamberlain trompa son attendre et Churchill dut patienter encore une année.

1 September 1939. Inhabitants of Warsaw read
Hitler's ultimatum, posted all over the city. The choice
offered to the Poles was capitulation or invasion.
The next day the city was bombed by the Luftwaffe.

1. September 1939. Die Einwohner Warschaus
erfahren auf Plakaten von Hitlers Ultimatum:
Kapitulation oder Invasion. Bereits am nächsten
Tag wurde die Stadt bombardiert.

1er septembre 1939. Des habitants de Varsovie lisent
l'ultimatum de Hitler, affiché sur tous les murs de
la ville, qui proposait aux Polonais la capitulation ou
l'invasion. Le lendemain, la ville fut bombardée par
la Luftwaffe.

September 1938.
Chamberlain arrives
at Heston airport on
his return from
Munich. He believed
it was 'peace in
our time'. 'Our time'
lasted 12 months.

September 1938.
Chamberlains
Ankunft auf dem
Flughafen Heston.
Nach seiner Rück-
kehr aus München
vertrat er die Über-
zeugung, es herrsche
„Frieden in unserer
Zeit". Dieser dauerte
jedoch nur 12
Monate.

Septembre 1938.
L'arrivée de
Chamberlain à
l'aéroport de
Heston, à son retour
de Munich. Il
pensait avoir obtenu
la « paix pour
longtemps ». Elle
dura 12 mois.

Paris newspapers announce the outbreak of World War II. Unlike its predecessor, it was greeted with resignation rather than enthusiasm.

Pariser Zeitungen verkünden den Ausbruch des Zweiten Weltkriegs. Entgegen der vorherigen Kriegs-erklärung rief diese bei der Bevölkerung keinen Enthusias-mus, sondern nur Resignation hervor.

Les journaux parisiens annoncent le début de la Seconde Guerre mondiale. Contraire-ment à la précé-dente, celle-ci fut accueillie avec résignation plutôt qu'enthousiasme.

Eight hundred evacuee children gather on Ealing Broadway station, West London, 1939. They were on their way to the country, where they would be safe from bombing raids. After the comparative inactivity of the 'Phoney War', many of them returned to London in time for the Blitz.

Achthundert Kinder sammeln sich auf dem Bahnhof von Ealing Broadway in West-London, 1939. Zum Schutz vor Bombenangriffen wurden sie aufs Land verschickt. Als der Krieg in der Folgezeit vergleichsweise ruhig verlief, kehrten viele Kinder nach London zurück – gerade zu dem Zeitpunkt als der Blitz begann.

Rassemblement de huit cents enfants à la gare d'Ealing Broadway, à l'Ouest de Londres, 1939. Ils furent évacués à la campagne pour être à l'abri des bombardements. Après le calme relatif de la « drôle de guerre », beaucoup d'enfants regagnèrent Londres, en fait peu avant le Blitz.

December 1938.
The first of 5,000
Jewish and non-
Aryan refugees from
Germany arrive at
the port of Harwich.

Dezember 1938. Die
ersten von insgesamt
5.000 jüdischen und
nicht-arischen deut-
schen Flüchtlingen
treffen in der
englischen Hafen-
stadt Harwich ein.

Décembre 1938.
Arrivée au port de
Harwich, Angleterre,
d'une petite fille,
la première des
5 000 réfugiés
juifs et non aryens
en provenance
d'Allemagne.

Corporal White, of the 1st City of London Regiment, marries Miss A Nock at a sandbagged Islington Registry Office, 1939.

Stabsunteroffizier White vom 1. Londoner Stadtregiment und Miss A. Nock heiraten in dem von Sandsäcken geschützten Standesamt von Islington, 1939.

Le Caporal-Chef White du 1er Régiment de la Cité de Londres épouse Mlle Nock à la mairie d'Islington, tapissée de sacs de sable, 1939.

September 1939.
Nurses stand on
sandbags that cover
a London hospital.
The photograph
was taken by
Frederick Ramage.

September 1939.
Frederick Ramage
nahm diese beiden
Krankenschwestern
auf, die auf einem
mit Sandsäcken
abgedeckten
Krankenhausdach
stehen.

Septembre 1939.
Des infirmières
debout sur les sacs
de sable qui
recouvrent un
hôpital de Londres.
Cette photographie
fut prise par
Frederick Ramage.

A London ARP (Air Raid Precautions) warden, off duty, 1939. Wardens were often seen as figures of fun, the butt of many comedians' humour.

Ein Londoner Luftschutzwart bei einer Teepause, 1939. Luft-schutzwarte waren häufig Opfer von Hohn und Spott und dienten vielen Komödianten als Zielscheibe ihrer Attacken.

Quartier libre pour un préposé à la défense passive à Londres, 1939. Ces préposés furent souvent l'objet de plaisanteries et la cible de nombreux humoristes.

Sandbags at the seashore – Whitley Bay, Northumberland, 1939. Sandbags were needed all over Britain, and soldiers, civilians, Boy Scouts and schoolchildren were all recruited to fill the bags with sand and meet the demand.

Am Strand von Whitley Bay in Northumberland werden Sandsäcke gefüllt, 1939. Da in ganz Großbritannien Sandsäcke benötigt wurden, halfen Soldaten, Zivilisten, Pfadfinder und sogar Schulkinder beim Füllen.

Sacs de sable à la plage, Whitley Bay, Northumberland, 1939. Il fallait des sacs de sable pour toute la Grande-Bretagne. Pour faire face à la demande, on recruta des soldats, des civils, des scouts et des écoliers.

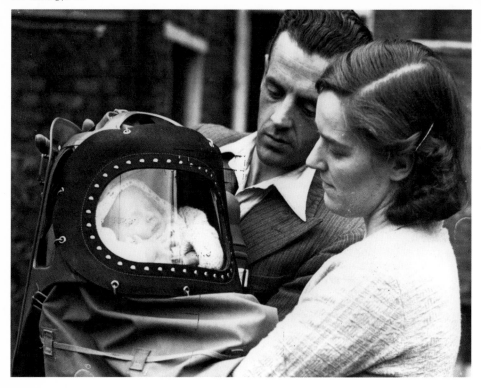

14 September 1939. Neville Mooney, the first baby to
be born in London after the declaration of war, arrives home
from hospital. His gas mask was the special baby model.

14. September 1939. Das erste nach Kriegsbeginn in London
geborene Baby, Neville Mooney, verläßt mit seinen Eltern
das Krankenhaus. Zum Schutz trägt es das Babymodell einer
Gasmaske.

14 septembre 1939. Neville Mooney, le premier bébé né
à Londres après la déclaration de la guerre, arrive à la
maison après sa sortie de l'hôpital. Son masque à gaz était
un modèle spécialement conçu pour les bébés.

An orderly
evacuation of office
workers on their
way to the shelters,
1939. Drills like
this were frequent,
and intended to
boost morale.

Büroangestellte
begeben sich
vorschriftsgemäß in
die zugewiesenen
Bunker, 1939.
Solche regelmäßig
durchgeführten
Übungen sollten der
Bevölkerung
moralischen Auftrieb
geben und die Angst
nehmen.

Evacuation
disciplinée
d'employés de
bureau vers leurs
abris, 1939. De tels
exercices étaient
fréquents et destinés
à remonter le moral
de la population.

July 1939. Interior
decoration – Mr
Barlow, a marine
store dealer, puts
some finishing
touches to his
air-raid shelter.

Juli 1939. Innenaus-
stattung – Mr.
Barlow, ein Händler
für Marinebedarf,
gibt seinem
Luftschutzbunker
den letzten Schliff.

Juillet 1939.
Décoration intérieure
– M. Barlow, un
marchand d'articles
de pêche, apporte les
dernières finitions à
son abri antiaérien.

August 1939.
External
ornamentation
– Mr and Mrs
Joseph Pigot tend
the pots of flowering
plants that cover
their shelter.

August 1939.
Außenschmuck –
Mr. und Mrs. Joseph
Pigot hegen und
pflegen die Blüten-
pracht auf dem Dach
ihres Bunkers.

Août 1939.
Décoration
extérieure. M. et
Mme Joseph Pigot
entretiennent les
pots de fleurs qui
décorent le dessus
de leur abri.

Anti-bomb blast precautions, 1939. Sheets of cellophane are pasted
over windows to prevent the glass splintering in an explosion.
Cellophane was a new invention, originally intended as a wrapping
for food.

Sicherheitsvorkehrungen gegen Bombenexplosionen, 1939.
Fenster werden mit Cellophan-Folien beklebt, um die Scheiben vor
dem Zersplittern zu schützen. Die Neuentwicklung Cellophan
war eigentlich als Verpackungsmaterial für Lebensmittel gedacht.

Précautions anti-bombes, 1939. Pose de cellophane pour éviter que
le verre ne vole en éclats en cas d'explosion. Le cellophane était une
invention nouvelle, destinée initialement à l'emballage des aliments.

Quality control at a blackout material factory, 1939. The blackout had
to be thick and impenetrable. It was said that the merest glow or chink
of light would be enough to guide enemy bombers to their target.

Qualitätskontrolle in einer Fabrik für Verdunkelungsstoffe, 1939. Der
Stoff mußte schwer sein und durfte nicht den kleinsten Lichtschimmer
nach außen dringen lassen, der den feindlichen Bombenflugzeugen
ein Ziel geboten hätte.

Contrôle de qualité, 1939. Cette usine fabrique un tissu épais et
opaque, spécialement conçu pour le couvre-feu. On racontait que la
moindre lueur ou tâche de lumière suffirait à guider les bombardiers
ennemis vers leur cible.

Index

How to buy or license a picture from this book

The pictures in this book are drawn from the extensive archives of The Hulton Getty Picture Collection, originally formed in 1947 as the Hulton Press Library. The Collection contains approximately 15 million images, some of which date from the earliest days of photography. It includes original material from leading press agencies – Topical Press, Keystone, Central Press, Fox Photos and General Photographic Agency as well as from *Picture Post*, the *Daily Express* and the *Evening Standard*.

Picture Licensing Information

To license the pictures listed below please call Getty Images **+ 44 171 266 2662** or email **info@getty-images.com** your picture selection with the page/reference numbers.

Hulton Getty Online

All of the pictures listed below and countless others are available via Hulton Getty Online at: **http://www.hultongetty.com**

Buying a print

For details of how to purchase exhibition-quality prints call The Hulton Getty Picture Gallery **+ 44 171 376 4525**

Acknowledgements

Slava Katamidze 278

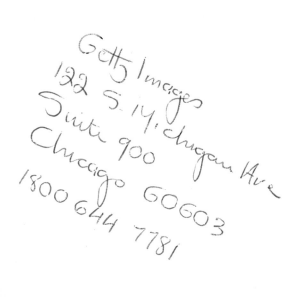

". . . this Holy Terror from Baltimore is splendidly and exultantly and contagiously alive. He calls you a swine, and an imbecile, and he increases your will to live."

—WALTER LIPPMANN

THE IMPOSSIBLE

H. L. Mencken

A Selection of His Best
Newspaper Stories

Edited by
MARION ELIZABETH RODGERS

With a Foreword by
GORE VIDAL

ANCHOR BOOKS
DOUBLEDAY
NEW YORK LONDON TORONTO SYDNEY AUCKLAND

An Anchor Book
PUBLISHED BY DOUBLEDAY
a division of Bantam Doubleday Dell Publishing Group, Inc.
666 Fifth Avenue, New York, New York 10103

ANCHOR BOOKS, DOUBLEDAY and the portrayal of an anchor
are trademarks of Doubleday, a division of Bantam Doubleday Dell
Publishing Group, Inc.

The Impossible H. L. Mencken is published simultaneously in a hardcover edition by
Doubleday, a division of Bantam Doubleday Dell Publishing Group, Inc.

Library of Congress Cataloging-in-Publication Data

Mencken, H. L. (Henry Louis), 1880–1956.
The impossible H. L. Mencken: a selection of his best newspaper stories
edited by Marion Elizabeth Rodgers.—1st ed.
p. cm.
I. Rodgers, Marion Elizabeth. II. Title.
PS3525.E43A6 1991
814′.52—dc20 91-284
CIP